The New Religious Studies Course for Catholic Schools

Dr Anthony Towey & Philip Robinson

EDUQAS
ROUTE B

redemptorist publications

Published by Redemptorist Publications
Alphonsus House, Chawton, Hampshire, GU34 3HQ, UK
Tel. +44 (0)1420 88222, Fax. +44 (0)1420 88805
Email rp@rpbooks.co.uk, www.rpbooks.co.uk

A registered charity limited by guarantee
Registered in England 3261721
Copyright © Redemptorist Publications 2016
First published September 2016

Text by Anthony Towey, Philip Robinson and Dr Paul Rowan
Edited by Anthony Towey
Designed by Emma Hagan
Cover illustration by Tree Behrens

The image on the cover represents the Covenants, or promises, between God and humankind, many of which are held in common by the Abrahamic Faiths.

The three languages, Latin, Arabic and Hebrew, here represent the three strands of the Abrahamic Tradition. The words are virtues of the faiths. The words in Latin are Faith and Mercy; in Hebrew, Loving Kindness, Covenant and Holy; in Arabic, Wisdom, Kindness and Self-Control.

The first Covenant is between God and humanity in Adam and Eve. The apple branch refers to the Edenic Covenant which was broken when Adam and Eve ate fruit from the tree of knowledge. The fig leaves represent the curses pronounced when God finds Adam and Eve hiding in the garden wearing fig leaves.

The seven lines refer to the rainbow from the second Covenant, known as the Noahic Covenant. God makes a promise to Noah after the flood to never again submerge the land with water.

The third Covenant is the Abrahamic Covenant. After being tested by God, Abraham is promised descendants as many as the stars (represented by the dots). Abraham means 'father of the people' and he is recognised as a very important figure in Christianity, Islam and Judaism.

The next Covenant is with Moses, who led the Jews out of slavery in Egypt to the Promised Land. On Mount Sinai he received the Law from God, commonly known as the Ten Commandments, or the Law of Moses.

God's Covenant with David refers to land and kingship. God promised that David's kingdom would be established for ever through David's descendants. Christians believe that Jesus is the fulfilment of this promise.

Tree Behrens

Nihil obstat: Fr Terry Tastard, Censor
Imprimatur: His Eminence Cardinal Vincent Nichols,
Archbishop of Westminster
August 2016

The *Nihil Obstat* and *Imprimatur* are a declaration that a book or pamphlet is considered to be free from doctrinal or moral error. It is not implied that those who have granted the *Nihil Obstat* and *Imprimatur* agree with the contents, opinions or statements expressed.

ISBN 978085231 4791

The New GCSE Religious Studies Course for Catholic Schools

Dr Anthony Towey & Philip Robinson

Contents

The eventual book version of this Unit will come complete with extension topics, memory exercises and sample assessments. The latter are already available from the Eduqas website **www.eduqas.co.uk**

Online resources avaliable at www.rp-education.co.uk

Foundational Catholic Theology

CORE IDEA

The Three-Legged Stool of Scripture, Tradition and Magisterium!

Catholic thinking about God ('theology') emerges out of a three-way conversation between: (1) the Bible; (2) wise and ordinary people such as saints, theologians, religious thinkers, philosophers and scientists; and (3) popes and bishops.

KEY TERMS

Theology = literally, 'God-words', or 'God-talk'. As a subject, it is the study of God and things to do with God (such as his relationship with human beings).

Revelation = how God communicates with humanity.

Tradition = inspired wisdom captured in the words, customs and lives of Christians.

Scripture = **the Bible** = the inspired collection of writings sacred to Christians.

Introduction

Before We Get Going: Catholic 'God-talk'

To do well in this course you need to know lots about Catholic Christianity – and the first thing you need to know is how this Christian tradition does its thinking so that you can compare different views and different arguments well.

Tradition and Community

The first thing to note in Catholic thinking is the importance of tradition. 'Tradition' is a word that comes from the Latin word *tradito*, which means something handed on or passed on. Consider football as a tradition: if we are attracted to football, it is rarely through reading a rule book or coaching manual. Rather, we are attracted to the sport by watching a football match on TV or at a stadium, or by playing it at school or in the park. We might become a fan of a particular team and we might become aware of its traditions – the colours it plays in or even the style it is known for. These things help create a sense of belonging and community.

Tradition, Scripture and Magisterium

Jesus is at the heart of Christian tradition. Jesus passed on his teachings by word and example, in fact by his whole way of life. In turn, the Apostles handed on this revelation in the following definite ways – all of which help to hold the community together in unity:

- By living: 'they handed on, by the spoken word of their preaching, by the example they gave, by the institutions they established, what they themselves had received – whether from the lips of Christ, from his way of life and his works, or whether they had learned it at the prompting of the Holy Spirit.' (Dei Verbum 7).

- By writing: 'by those apostles and other men associated with the apostles who, under the inspiration of the same Holy Spirit, committed the message of salvation to writing' (Dei Verbum 7). This is how we come to have the Gospels and other books from the New Testament part of the Bible.

- By teaching authority: there were inevitable disagreements from the beginning– such as whether Christians who were not originally Jews should be circumcised. By making big decisions on questions like this (see Acts of the Apostles 15), the leaders of the Church were exercising 'teaching authority'. This has a posh name – Magisterium – which comes from the Latin for 'teacher'.

> **Magisterium** = the teaching role entrusted to bishops in union with the Pope.
>
> **Inspiration** = 'God-breathed' – the way the Holy Spirit works through human beings.

This is why Paul writes to the Christians in Thessalonica: 'Stand firm, then, brothers, and keep the traditions that we taught you, whether by word of mouth or by letter' (2 Thessalonians 2:15). So, unlike some Christian groups who only pay attention to the Bible, Catholics believe that the Word of God – the Revelation, the Gospel of Jesus Christ – is handed on to others from age to age not just through the writings of the Bible, but also by a living Tradition and by Magisterium – its teaching authority.

Vatican II on Tradition, Scripture and Magisterium

According to Church teaching: 'It is clear, therefore, that sacred tradition, Sacred Scripture and the teaching authority of the Church, in accord with God's most wise design, are so linked and joined together that one cannot stand without the others, and that all together and each in its own way under the action of the one Holy Spirit contribute effectively to the salvation of souls' (Dei Verbum 10).

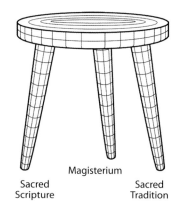

Magisterium

Sacred Scripture

Sacred Tradition

G. K. Chesterton once said that health and sanity require balance – we can have too much food or too little food, too much exercise or too little exercise. Physical, mental and spiritual health all require finding a reasonable balance. When Catholics think about God (theology), they want to do it in a healthy, sane and balanced way.

- Catholic theology can be thought of as thinking about God and his relationship to human beings on the three-legged stool of Scripture, Tradition and Magisterium. The three legs ensure that the Church's thinking is more balanced and much healthier! Three legs allow for a steadier foundation. We don't need to ask which of the three is most important – all three are gifts from God to help us understand him and his will for us.

Engage Brain: conscience and the aims of this course

This explanation about how Catholic scholars think is not meant to wipe your database. The very opposite. The Catholic tradition involves faith and reason, and this RE GCSE course involves 'engaging brain'. You have to know why Catholics, other Christians and indeed non-believers come to their conclusions. You need to know the arguments, but you are not being forced to agree with them.

Why? The Church confidently believes and proposes its teaching to its members and to the world. However, as Pope St John Paul II said in a document concerning the spreading of the Gospel message: '*The Church proposes: she imposes nothing*. She respects individuals and cultures, and she honours the sanctuary of conscience' (Redemptoris Missio 39; italics in original).

This is important not just in society but also in school. The RE classroom is a place of mutual respect, and in the exploration of religious beliefs, all views should be treated with sensitivity. Through this dialogue everyone can be enriched such that we can travel through this life together and make the world a better place.

Discussion

Does your school have any special traditions? Your family? Your town? Your country? What are they? How do they bring people together? Is there anyone in charge of the tradition? Are there any documents written down?

Unit 1.1: Catholic Beliefs about the Origin of the Universe and the Concept of 'creatio ex nihilo'

CORE IDEA

The cosmos/universe has a meaning, and therefore a creator. This is the concept of *creatio ex nihilo* (creation out of nothing) as explored in the writing of St Augustine of Hippo (Confessions XII, 7).

INTRODUCTION

- Catholic thinking is a quest for truth – in relation to creation, humanity and God.

- While ultimately it concludes that these truths are most clearly revealed in a life lived – that of Jesus – it also acknowledges that it is an aspect of our dignity as humans to wonder and to question. And there is no more fundamental question than to ask why there is anything to wonder at in the first place!

  - Is the universe the product of cosmic chance, a magic molecule, a Big Bang, a steady state or one aspect of a multiverse?
  - Is the universe the gift of a divine Creator, an expression of cosmic mega-power, or an invitation to love?

- If you're looking for 'Big Questions', they don't get much bigger than this! So in this first theme we are going to explore what the Catholic Church teaches about the origins and meaning of the universe, the world, human beings and the relationships between humans, the rest of creation and God, the Creator of all.

Nature and Meaning: G. K. Chesterton

Catholic journalist G. K. Chesterton (1874–1936) said that if we look at the world, we notice that 'it seems to proceed by certain rules, [and we see] in the growth of flowers a green architecture that builds itself without visible hand. There seems to be a design, a purpose, an intention to produce the flowers, plants, trees and other things in the world.'

Gilbert K. Chesterton (1909) by Ernest Herbert Mills

Therefore, says Chesterton, many wise thinkers have concluded 'that the world had a plan as the tree seemed to have a plan … Most men, including the wisest men, have come to the conclusion that the world has such a final purpose and therefore such a first cause' (The Everlasting Man, Part 2, Conclusion).

KEY TERMS

Origins = the beginnings of something, where it came from.

Purpose = the meaning of something, the plan behind it.

Eternal = without beginning or end.

Transcendent = beyond time and space.

First Cause = the reality that caused everything to exist.

Creatio ex nihilo = creation out of nothing.

Omnipotent = all-powerful.

Omnibenevolent = all-loving.

'A final purpose' is the overall plan or meaning to the world/universe/cosmos. Chesterton says, 'I had always felt life first as a story: and if there is a story there is a story-teller' (Orthodoxy, Chapter 4). Catholics refer to this person, this author of the story of the world, as 'God'. God is the origin of the world, the 'first cause' or Creator. Christians, Jews and Muslims all call God the Creator, the One who gives the world its meaning.

Creation out of Nothing: St Augustine

An early thinker in the Catholic tradition who grappled with the idea of the origins of the universe was Saint Augustine of Hippo (AD 354–430).

There are several things Augustine introduces here which we will explore more in later units:

Saint Augustine in his Study by Sandro Botticelli, 1494, Uffizi Gallery

> … you, O Lord … made something in the Beginning, which is of yourself, in your Wisdom, which is born of your own substance, and you created this thing out of nothing. You created heaven and earth but you did not make them of your own substance. If you had done so, they would have been equal to your only-begotten Son, and therefore to yourself, and justice could in no way admit that what was not of your own substance should be equal to you. But besides yourself, O God, who are Trinity in Unity, Unity in Trinity, there was nothing from which you could make heaven and earth. Therefore you must have created them from nothing, the one great, the other small. For there is nothing that you cannot do. You are good and all that you make must be good, both the great Heaven of Heavens and this little earth. You were, and besides you nothing was. From nothing, then, you created heaven and earth, distinct from one another; the one close to yourself, the other close to being nothing; the one surpassed only by yourself, the other little more than nothing.
>
> (St Augustine, Confessions XII, 7, in Augustine: Confessions and Enchiridion, edited by Albert Cook Outler, Library of Christian Classics)

God is …

- Eternal: 'You were, and besides you nothing was': in the beginning, before the creation of the universe, before time and space exists, only God exists. Catholics (and all Christians) believe that God is eternal, without beginning or end, the ultimate reality, the only reality that has always existed, that simply is. See Exodus 3:14, where God tells Moses his name: 'I AM'.

- Transcendent: God is also transcendent (beyond time and space). God is not part of the universe, on top of a mountain or living in the sky, but neither is God 'absent from' creation – the whole cosmos is kept in existence by God's existence.

- Trinity: There is something that is 'born of' God's 'own substance'. This 'something' is God's 'only-begotten Son'. Augustine here refers to it as the 'Trinity in Unity, Unity in Trinity'.

- Creator: God created 'heaven and earth'. Every Sunday in the Nicene Creed Christians profess their belief in God the Father Almighty as 'maker of heaven and earth, of all things visible and invisible'.

- Not a Creature: 'You created heaven and earth but you did not make them of your own substance.' In the ancient world, many people worshipped aspects of nature as if they were gods – for example, Thor was a Thunder god, Dagon a fish god, Venus a Love goddess. Augustine says it flat out: Creation is not equal to God.

- Supreme Being: This means that no part of creation is equal in greatness to God: 'justice could in no way admit that what was not of your own substance should be equal to you.' Because creation is not God himself, it can be explored and used by human beings.

- Omnipotent: God was able to create something out of nothing (*ex nihilo*) because God is omnipotent (all-powerful): 'there is nothing that you cannot do'.

- Omnibenevolent: God is also good (or loving): 'You are good and all that you make must be good'. He loves creation into being. Creation comes into being out of God's love. The fact that there is a universe is a sign of God's love. Creation is 'loved into existence' – it is good because God is good.

Discussion

- What rules (or laws of nature) are there in the world or in the wider universe/cosmos?
- How do you think they got there? Why do you think they got there?
- If there are 'laws' of nature, who put the laws there? Does there have to be a 'lawgiver' behind the laws?
- Do you think there is a final purpose – that is, an ultimate meaning – to the world, or to the universe/cosmos?
- Do you think your life has a meaning?
- If there is an ultimate, overall meaning, how come? Who decides what that meaning is or should be? Is there, as Chesterton says, a person behind the meaning? Is there some overall story being told as the universe unfolds? Is there a storyteller?

Unit 1.2 and 1.9: Genesis Creation Accounts – Catholic and fundamentalist understandings

CORE IDEA

We will look at the two Creation accounts in Genesis chapters 1 and 2 to show the similarities and differences between the Catholic and fundamentalist Christian (literalist) ways of reading Scripture and see what consequences there are for interpreting the meaning of those passages.

It is clear that Augustine and G. K. Chesterton are greatly influenced by the Bible in their understanding of Creation. However, it is SO important to realise that neither of them made the mistake of reading the Bible as a scientific document or a literal description of cosmic origins. It is very important to make this distinction because some people think that the Pope, bishops and Catholics in general have a fundamentalist approach to Scripture, which is simply not true.

SIMILARITIES: Both Catholics and Christian fundamentalists: believe in God; believe that the authors of the biblical books are inspired by God; believe that the books of the Bible contain God's revelation; and believe that the books of the Bible are the living Word of God that helps us face life today.

DIFFERENCE: Catholics believe that if we are to understand better the Bible, and therefore what God reveals through it in order to help us face life today, then we need to take into consideration the context in which the Bible's books were written. Fundamentalist Christians do not believe this – they believe that God's revelation in the Bible is plain and obvious from simply reading the words.

To show how this difference pans out, let's take the famous first two chapters of the Book of Genesis.

Genesis 1:1 – 2:4a and Genesis 2:4b–25 – two Creation accounts

Genesis (meaning 'beginnings' or 'origins') is the first book of the Bible. The first chapter is an ancient meditation on the creation of the cosmos, while most of chapter 2 is a different account about the creation of human beings.

Different Authors, Same Mystery

- From Chaos to Harmony: Genesis 1:1 – 2:4a is complete as a story. God creates everything that exists, including human beings, over the course of six days, and rests on the seventh day; this inspired author communicates the message that the cosmos is in harmony.

- From Loneliness to Communion: Another author has given us Genesis 2:4b–25. This is a meditation on human beings. It is a parable of Paradise which paints a picture of how by our very nature we belong to Creation, we belong to God and we belong to each other.

KEY TERMS

Aetiology = a symbolic story describing why things are the way they are.

Category mistake = reading one literary form in the Bible as though it were another literary form.

Creationism = a literalist understanding of the origins of the cosmos and human beings, as described in Genesis 1–2.

- Catholic Christians are called to look into the depth of these accounts to discern the underlying meaning. Through these inspired authors aspects of God are revealed – 'all-powerful, transcendent, benevolent' – but truths about us are revealed also: that we are made in the image of God (Genesis 1:27); that we have a role in Creation; that we only have life through God's kindness; and that we are lonely without each other (Genesis 2:7–24).

- Fundamentalist Christians are brought up to believe that Genesis was written from start to finish by Moses and would therefore try hard to explain or reconcile the differences between these two passages, since their more literalist reading would demand that.

Different Forms – Same Message

A second thing Catholics note is the literary form of the texts in these two chapters. Genesis 1 can be regarded as an ancient meditation on the cosmos, while Genesis 2 can be viewed as a symbolic parable about humanity – both of which convey the deepest truths about God, our world, ourselves.

The Christian fundamentalist would say that since Genesis is written from God's point of view, this can be regarded as a historical account of what actually happened at the beginning of time. Catholics would call this a category mistake – a basic misreading of a text which is more like prayer, poetry, psalm and parable than a 'this happened, then that' sequence of events.

Signs, not Science

To read these passages as science is another category mistake. Catholics do not read this story as an alternative to the Big Bang Theory that implies that the universe was created in six days, with God then taking a day off to get his breath back. Nor is the story of Adam and Eve incompatible with Darwin's theory of evolution. No – the authors of Genesis are not trying to do what Newton, Darwin or Einstein did when asking scientific questions of how the universe works; instead, the core of their question is why the universe is. Creation is a sign that God has created all things out of love and that he has created humanity to participate in that love – of Creation, of God and of each other.

Again, a more fundamentalist Christian reading would involve an attempt to defend the literal interpretation of the Creation in six days (this interpretation is called creationism) and the drawing of woman from the rib of man. As we shall see later, this would clearly mean that a fundamentalist reading would have problems with the notion of the Big Bang cosmogony or with Darwin's theory of the evolutionary origins of the human and other species.

Time and Timing

Catholics interpret the sequence of 'days' as indicating that God is the Creator even of time, not that Creation literally took six days. Even though the Bible itself teaches that to the Lord, 'a thousand years are a single day' (Psalm 90:4; see also 2 Peter 3:8), most fundamentalists are inclined to take the text literally. Then, by calculating the ages of people in the Bible, they conclude that Creation took place in 4004 BC, despite the discovery of fossils and other contrary evidence.

Catholic Summary

The wisest theologians, scientists and scholars have always realised that intelligence and subtlety are required for a fuller understanding of the Bible. Forgetting this can lead to simplistic interpretations of the sacred texts and endless misunderstandings.

Discussion

- Imagine a thousand years from now someone reading an article about 'Ant and Dec – Superstars'. How would they know whether it was referring to cosmic or comic realities? What other evidence would they need in order to decide?
- What are the main differences between Catholic and fundamentalist views on Genesis?
- What is the Bible trying to show in these first chapters in comparison with what science is trying to do?
- We have God-given minds and we are full of questions, but before we get too cocky, have we considered what questions these texts are asking us??? #justsaying

Ant and Dec.
Featureflash Photo Agency / Shutterstock.com

Unit 1.3: Genesis and the Big Bang

CORE IDEA

In this unit we will explore the relationship between the Catholic view of Creation, the Big Bang Theory and the views of Stephen Hawking.

The Big Bang Theory:
Einstein, Hoyle, Lemaître and Hawking

- This idea of a unique and explosive beginning to the cosmos out of 'a singular moment' – a singular dense point containing all of the universe's matter and energy, which is then thrown outwards – is called the *Big Bang theory*. What a lot of people do not realise is that this theory was first put forward *not by Stephen Hawking, but by a Catholic priest, Father Georges Lemaître*. In 1933, when Einstein heard the details of Lemaître's theory, he said, 'This is the most beautiful and satisfactory explanation of creation to which I have ever listened.'

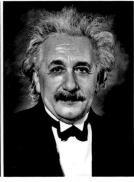

Georges Lemaître (1894–1966), Belgian priest, astronomer and professor of physics at the Catholic University of Leuven, 1933. (Left) and Albert Einstein, 1935

KEY TERMS

Cosmology = study of the cosmos/universe.

Big Bang = the idea that the universe originated in an explosion of light, matter and energy that created time and space.

Cosmogony = explanations of the beginnings of the cosmos/universe.

- The phrase 'Big Bang', now part and parcel of accepted scientific wisdom, was actually intended originally as a sarcastic insult by the astronomer Fred Hoyle, who disliked Lemaître's theory. He claimed that many scientists only liked the theory because it was 'deep within the psyche of most scientists to believe in the first page of Genesis'. Hoyle was clearly concerned that some people might associate a 'Big Bang' with the line God speaks in Genesis (1:3): 'Let there be light'. What Hoyle originally intended as a put-down ended up becoming the official title of the theory which remains the most approved scientific explanation for the beginnings of the cosmos!

- Why was a Catholic priest able to come up with this theory? Catholics have a more nuanced, less literalist approach to reading the Bible than do some other Christian groups. There is simply no contradiction for a Catholic between what Genesis says and what science says, because Genesis is theology, not science. The author of Genesis is saying *why* things are the way they are, *not how* things are the way they are. *Theology answers the question 'why?' Science answers the question 'how?'* The author of Genesis is trying to say that this wonderful, intelligible universe, which God invites us to explore scientifically with our God-given intelligence, had a beginning – the creative act of a loving and intelligent God who created everything out of nothing. If God chose to do that through the Big Bang, all well and good!

Stephen Hawking

- One of the most famous cosmologists living today is Stephen Hawking. As with Lemaître, his work has led him to wrestle with the philosophers of ancient Greece who believed that the universe had no beginning – it had always existed. In 1916, Albert Einstein's theory of relativity seemed to confirm this, and it was the position of many philosophers and scientists in the early part of the twentieth century; for example, Bertrand Russell (1872–1970) and Sir Fred Hoyle (1915–2001) held to a 'steady-state' theory of the cosmos, in which galaxies form every now and then out of created matter, and in which there is neither beginning nor end to reality.

- At one level Hawking has criticised Hoyle's theory, saying that scientific observations in the late twentieth and early twenty-first centuries do not support the idea of an everlasting, 'always there' universe. Hawking says that when we look closely at the number of galaxies and their stages of development, it seems to indicate that the universe is of a fairly specific age (roughly 14 billion years old). In other words, there is very strong evidence to support the theory that the universe had a one-off beginning – what Hawking calls a 'moment of singularity', a dense moment of energy, before which 'nothing' existed and out of which began the universe of time and space which we now know.

- However, the one thing on which Hawking and the Catholic Church would disagree with regard to the Big Bang theory concerns whether or not the theory implies that there is a Creator: Hawking says it doesn't, while, like Lemaître, the Church unsurprisingly says it does. In his 2010 book *The Grand Design*, Hawking says: 'Because there is a law such as gravity, the universe can and will create itself from nothing.' This is a confusing sentence to a Catholic. The Church would ask Hawking to clarify whether he means that the law of gravity is there prior to the existence of the universe. Because if there is a law of gravity that already exists and that is the reason for the universe, then he cannot say that the universe comes from nothing – gravity is not nothing!

Christian Critique: God is the Necessary Being

- At the risk of getting all theological, Christians would claim to be asking a more fundamental question than Hawking, in that how the universe came about is not as basic as why it came about. 'Why is there something rather than nothing?' is the question which ultimately led the leading atheist Anthony Flew to a belief in God. This is because all realities within the universe are contingent beings – they depend on something else. For example, you wouldn't be here without your parents. There must be something that is not dependent on anything – a First Cause, or necessary being. That means that gravity is a contingent reality and cannot be, as Hawking claims, the cause of the universe of which it is a part.

° Christian thinking identifies the necessary being as God – 'I Am who I Am' (Exodus 3:14). God is 'the One who Is' – the First and Final Cause of everything.

Discussion

Did You Know? Anthony Flew (1923-2010) was the Richard Dawkins of his day and spent many years questioning religious belief through his Falsification Principle. He eventually began to mistrust his conclusions based on mounting scientific evidence that the Universe was 'fine-tuned' for the emergence of humanity and by the Sound of Music argument where Maria sings: 'Nothing comes from nothing – nothing ever could'. He regarded 'multi-verse' theories of other parallel universes as particularly desperate. See *There is a God: How the World's most notorious Atheist changed his mind*, New York: Harpercollins, 2007.

✓ Differentiation & Discussion

'Science vs religion' or 'science and religion?
- Although the media would give the opposite impression, the Church has always been interested in scientific research and has always encouraged it, and some of the great figures in the history of science down to the present day have been/are Christian thinkers – for example, Copernicus, Newton, Kepler, Descartes, Pascal, Mendel, Lemaître, Jaki, Polkinghorne, Coyne, Consolmagno, Spitzer.
- It may seem odd, but some people attribute the growth of science in the West to the influence of theology. By pointing out that God made the earth and all the other bits of Creation, the author of Genesis does not regard Creation or any part of it as divine. That is why Christians do not worship any part of Creation but are free to explore it scientifically.
- Second, Genesis 1:1 says that Creation comes into being when God speaks his Word. 'Words' are essential to our 'understanding'. They follow a pattern and sign things – they have a logic. That means that all that exists is intelligible. Scientists can only start their research in the first place because the world is somehow 'understandable' – because God has stamped all of the universe with intelligibility at the Creation.

Why do you think there is a perception that religion and science are opposed? Where does it come from? Who benefits from this? What could be done to challenge this prejudice?

Unit 1.4: Genesis, Charles Darwin and Richard Dawkins

CORE IDEA

In this unit we will explore the relationship between Catholic beliefs about the purposeful creation of human beings and the scientific theory of evolution of Charles Darwin and Richard Dawkins.

Charles Darwin and the Evolutionary Theory of the Origins of Human Beings

- While visiting the Galapagos Islands, Charles Darwin (1809–82) noticed that there were variations in some of the characteristics found in animals of the same species on the different islands. He put this down to the variations in conditions on the different islands, saying that the animals had adapted to their different conditions. His theory of evolution attempted to explain how these variations come about – through the process of natural selection.

- Within a species, more offspring are produced than can survive, but offspring that have characteristics most suited to the environment will be the ones who thrive best and who go on to produce offspring themselves. Those with the characteristics least suited will not survive and will not reproduce so well. So the strongest and best-adapted survive, reproduce and pass on their characteristics to the next generation. Over a sufficient length of time a species will gradually evolve that is shaped by the characteristics that have been passed on. Herbert Spencer summarised this process as 'survival of the fittest'.

A couple of examples:

- Giraffes developed longer necks to help them reach higher food sources in the trees. Those who did not develop this longer neck died out.

  In parts of the world where cattle are used and milk/dairy products are a big part of the human diet, people have developed the enzyme required to break down milk. In regions where cows are not used much, human beings are lactose intolerant, lacking the enzyme.

- The evolutionary process is a very slow, gradual process in the history of our planet, and it continues here and now, today, in the same gradual way. It can be used to explain the close connections between species (e.g. between chimpanzees and humans). So, for Darwin, all animal species, including human beings, are the result of a natural and random process.

KEY TERMS

Organisms = living things such as animals, plants, fungi and bacteria.

Providence = God's governance of the universe.

Evolution = the theory that complex organisms developed from earlier simpler forms of life.

Evolution: 'natural and random' or 'natural and God-guided'?

- In the same way that Catholics can be fairly relaxed about the Big Bang, so too they can afford to be mellow about the alleged conflicts between Genesis 2 and Darwin. The Catholic approach to interpreting Scripture does not worry that God did not create the human species directly on something called a 'sixth day'. Nor does it try to square the theory of evolution from less-developed species with a complicated process involving soil (man), God's breath and a male rib (woman). The Catholic understanding of Genesis sees purpose – God's intention or loving plan – as the important factor, not length of time. If God wants to create human beings, who says the process he uses can't take 14 billion years and involve a Big Bang and evolution?

- As we saw in Unit 1.3, in Genesis we are dealing with theology, not science, *answering 'why?', not 'how?'* Therefore, Charles Darwin's basic idea that all species on earth, including the human species, have evolved (literally, 'unrolled') from simpler life forms over millions of years can be welcomed, not dismissed, by Catholics because there still needed to be something there in the first place, at the beginning, in order for it to be rolled out eventually. So, whereas science will emphasise the *how* – the natural and random process of evolution – theology emphasises the *why* – namely, that these processes are part of God's loving providence.

Pope St John Paul II on Evolution

Several popes, beginning with Pope Pius XII in 1950, have taught that there is no conflict between Darwin's theory and the Catholic understanding of God's deliberate, purposeful creation of human beings. On 22 October 1996, in his Message to the Pontifical Academy of Sciences: On Evolution, Saint John Paul II wrote:

'… In his encyclical Humani Generis (1950), my predecessor Pius XII has already affirmed that there is no conflict between evolution and the doctrine of the faith regarding man and his vocation … In order to mark out the limits of their own proper fields, theologians and those working on the exegesis of the Scripture need to be well informed regarding the results of the latest scientific research.'

Here, Saint John Paul II is emphasising that the Bible has to be read carefully, not simplistically, and that science contributes to the Church's wisdom and understanding. He goes on to say that since 1950, further discoveries in the natural sciences and other fields of study tend to suggest that evolution is a theory of great merit which advances our understanding.

'… Taking into account the scientific research of the era, and also the proper requirements of theology, the encyclical Humani Generis treated the doctrine of 'evolutionism' as a serious hypothesis, worthy of investigation and serious study … Today, more than a half-century after the appearance of that encyclical, some new findings lead us toward the recognition of evolution as more than an hypothesis. In fact it is remarkable that this theory has had progressively greater influence on the spirit of researchers, following a series of discoveries in different scholarly disciplines. The convergence in the results of these independent studies— which was neither planned nor sought—constitutes in itself a significant argument in favour of the theory.'

Neo-Darwinism and Richard Dawkins

- Study of the genes passed on from parent to child has led to a refinement of Darwin's theory, called Neo-Darwinism. One of the main figures in this research is Richard Dawkins. He has picked up on Darwin's idea of natural selection and adapted it with the idea of random and spontaneous genetic mutation. Living organisms, including human beings, have very complex genetic codes. Whenever a new organism/ species emerges, sometimes random genetic codes slip in. Some of these help the individual of the species to survive, while others make no difference to that survival.

- Dawkins, a committed atheist, understands the universe to be a place in which biological impulses alone drive life forward. There is no Creator God who has a purpose, a plan or a design for the universe: '... all life, all intelligence, all creativity and all "design" anywhere in the universe is the direct or indirect product of Darwinian natural selection ... Design cannot precede evolution and therefore cannot underlie the universe.'

- He sees the eventual arrival of life on earth as inevitable because of the genetic foundations for that life. Genes are little packets of information, programs that are struggling to survive. This struggle to survive is worked out in the process of evolution. Human beings, then, are genes locked up in living bodies, 'survival machines', genes that merely seek survival for the human species. Because humans are just packets of genes trying to survive, Dawkins says that there is no such thing as a soul, nor is there any evidence of one.

Some Catholic Reflections on Dawkins' Position and the Creation of Human Beings

- First, a Catholic might ask Dawkins how the universe first came into existence. Something has to exist before a life force can instinctively be driven forward through natural selection. In other words, no matter how complex the universe has been in the past, is today and will be in the future, we are once again forced to ask: 'Why is there something rather than nothing?' How did all this complexity begin?

- Second, a Catholic might also ask Dawkins how the purpose-carrying genetic codes which gave rise to the survival/self-reproduction instinct which he sees in living species could come from mere matter, in which there is no sense of purpose/plan/design.

- Third, a Catholic might not necessarily see a conflict between a God-created universe which is partly random. One of the great Catholic thinkers, St Thomas Aquinas, wrote: 'That Divine Providence does not exclude Fortune and Chance' (*Summa contra Gentiles*, III, 74, 1). From a limited human perspective, things might look random, but God ultimately guarantees the harmony of all creation (see Romans 8).

- Fourth, with regard to the soul, Catholics would say that science is not in a position to say anything about souls, because souls are not the type of thing science studies. Dawkins' area of expertise – physical/material biology – is not able to study spiritual/immaterial souls, and when Dawkins dismisses the idea of a soul, he is speaking not as a scientist, but as a philosopher. Spirit cannot evolve from matter. Molecules do not produce self-awareness, thought, free will and love. The soul is a different dimension of reality – spiritual, another world, a share in the life of God, God's breath in our body.

Consider the following quotation – the final words from Charles Darwin's *The Origin of the Species* (1959 edition):

'There is grandeur in this view of life, with its several powers, having been originally breathed into a few forms or into one; and that, whilst this planet has gone cycling on according to the fixed law of gravity, from so simple a beginning endless forms most beautiful and most wonderful have been, and are being, evolved.'

In the 1860 edition, Darwin inserted 'by the Creator'. Where did he put it? Why might he have done it? How far are his thoughts from those of these recent popes?

'On the one hand, there are so many scientific proofs in favour of evolution which appears to be a reality we can see and which enriches our knowledge of life and being as such. But on the other, the doctrine of evolution does not answer every query, especially the great philosophical question: where does everything come from? And how did everything start which ultimately led to man?'

Pope Benedict XVI

'The Big Bang, which nowadays is posited as the origin of the world, does not contradict the divine act of creating, but rather requires it. The evolution of nature does not contrast with the notion of Creation, as evolution presupposes the creation of beings that evolve. God "created human beings and let them develop according to the internal laws that he gave to each one so they would reach their fulfilment".'

Pope Francis

Unit 1.5: Saint Catherine of Siena on the *Imago Dei*

CORE IDEA

In this unit we recall the idea that humans are made in the image of God. With a little help from Saint Catherine of Siena, we explore how this sheds light on sacred destiny and the sanctity of human life.

Saint Catherine of Siena's Dialogue

Saint Catherine of Siena (1347–80) was a woman of deep spirituality, passionate in her desire to make people aware of their openness to God. She wrote a famous work about this called *The Dialogue of Divine Providence*, which is a conversation between God and a soul trying to make her way to God. Notice that she always refers to the soul in the Latin tradition as female.

> **The Dialogue of St Catherine of Siena 4.13**
>
> [The soul's] dignity is that of her creation, seeing that she is the image of God, and this has been given her by grace, and not as her due.
>
> In that same mirror of the goodness of God, the soul knows her own indignity, which is the consequence of her own fault.
>
> Wherefore, as a man more readily sees spots on his face when he looks in a mirror, so, the soul who, with true knowledge of self, rises with desire, and gazes with the eye of the intellect at herself in the sweet mirror of God, knows better the stains of her own face, by the purity which she sees in Him.
>
> 'Let us make man in our own image,' and this You did, oh eternal Trinity, that man might participate in everything belonging to You, the most high and eternal Trinity'...
>
> What made you establish man in so great a dignity? Certainly the incalculable love by which you have looked on your creature in yourself! You are taken with love for her; for by love indeed you created her, by love you have given her a being capable of tasting your eternal Good.

For her meditation on the *imago Dei*, Catherine uses the image of a reflection in a mirror. Why?

° **Origin:** So that we can reflect on the idea that we are not random organisms – our origin is in God, our life belongs to God alone.

° **Conscience:** Because we have God's love and truth in our lives, we also have an inner conscience that tells us when we have done wrong, when we come up short of our best selves.

° **Light to Love by:** Catherine says that the goodness of God shows us 'the stains on [our] face', like a mirror, or in the same way that the sun on the windscreen of a car shows up the dirt and the smudges!

KEY TERMS

Imago Dei = Latin for 'the image of God'.

Free will = humans can decide on their own actions.

Dignity = humans are worthy of respect.

Sanctity of life = human life is a gift from God and belongs to God alone.

Saint Catherine of Siena. From chiesa di Santa Maria del Rosario in Prati, Roma

- **Dignity and the Sanctity of Life:** This dignifies everyone. Despite being criticised for the bad company she kept, Catherine spent much of her life hanging around with the outcasts and sinners (as did Jesus). She knew that because God loved us enough to create us and make us in his image, we can be confident that he will pick us up to try again.

- **Destiny and the Sanctity of Life:** More than just respect in this life, *imago Dei* means that the true destiny of each human is to live in the eternal love of the Trinity. Life is thus sacred both in its origin and in its destiny.

G. K. Chesterton and Charles Taylor

Catherine was writing in a very different era from today. Two more recent thinkers offer different metaphors for what the idea of *imago Dei* means.

G. K. Chesterton (1874–1936) says the fact that pennies all bear the image of the monarch makes them all equal in value. He says that humans are also all equal in value because we all bear the image of the 'King of kings' – God.

Charles Taylor

Charles Taylor (b. 1931) (pictured, left) is a Catholic philosopher from Canada who writes a lot about the sacred nature of human life in this world. He talks of human beings having a 'porous self' – like a porous sponge that has holes and is open to moisture. Taylor believes that because we have a soul – the image of God within us – and we are porous, God can come into our lives. Unique among all creatures, humans are open to a higher world, the spiritual, the 'transcendent', God.

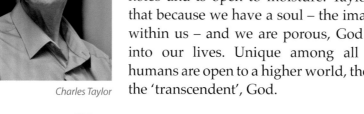

Discussion

- Consider this quote: 'Nature we seek to explain, humanity we seek to understand' (Wilhelm Dilthey). Just like Catherine of Siena, G. K. Chesterton and Charles Taylor, Dilthey (1833–1911) thought that in order to 'analyse' human beings, you almost need a different type of approach. Do you agree?
- Think of the different subjects you engage with at school – chemistry, PE, music, French, maths, literature, art. Do all of them ask the same type of question? Do they require the same skills? Do they all have the same teaching methods or objectives? How do they differ? Why? Can we ever understand ourselves as human beings without use of poetic images, metaphor and story?

Unit 1.6: Catholic and Other Christian Views on the Value of Human Life and on Abortion

CORE IDEA

In this unit we shall look at the Catholic understanding of the value of human life and explore how this shapes the Catholic attitude to abortion. We shall also look these issues from an Anglican perspective.

Catholic Beliefs about the Sanctity of Human Life

The Catholic Church teaches that everyone has the right to life and that 'Human life is sacred because from the beginning it involves the creative action of God and it remains for ever in a special relationship with the Creator, who is its sole end' (Catechism of the Catholic Church [CCC] 2258). Catholic views about the dignity of human life are rooted in their fundamental belief in the sanctity of human life. Catholics believe in the sanctity of human life for the following reasons:

° Origin: they see human life as a gift from the loving Creator God, who alone is Lord over life and death;

° Dignity: they believe that humans are made in God's image and are therefore persons with immortal souls;

° Destiny: they see the goal of this life as eternal joy with God in Heaven.

These factors influence the way Catholicism approaches the issue of abortion which it believes contravenes the most basic of human rights.

'Human life must be respected and protected absolutely from the moment of conception. From the first moment of his existence, a human being must be recognised as having the rights of a person – among which is the inviolable right of every innocent human being to life.'

CCC 2270

KEY TERMS

Pro-life = attitudes that are anti-abortion (an unborn's right to live).

Pro-choice = attitudes that are pro-abortion (a woman's right to choose).

Sanctity of life = life belongs to God.

The UK Law on Abortion

° UK law permits abortion before week 24 of pregnancy if two doctors agree that there is some risk to the mental or physical health of the mother or other children in the family if the pregnancy continued to term. Twenty-four weeks was decided as the limit beyond which abortion cannot take place because the latest medical opinion says that after then, babies are 'viable' – they can survive independently of the mother with intensive care.

° If there is a substantial risk that the baby will be born severely disabled, or if there is a serious risk of permanent mental or physical harm to the mother, there is no time limit on abortion.

The Catholic View on Abortion

- The debate about abortion has centred on the assumed conflict between the right to life of the unborn (the pro-life position) and the right of the woman to choose whether or not to continue a pregnancy (the pro-choice position).

- Consistent with its personalist approach to the ethics of human life, the Catholic Church teaches that abortion is morally wrong – it is the taking of an innocent human life.

  'Since the first century, the Church has affirmed the moral evil of every procured abortion. This teaching has not changed and remains unchangeable.'

  CCC 2271

- A 'procured abortion' is to be distinguished from a miscarriage, which is sometimes called a 'spontaneous abortion'. The long-standing and consistent wisdom which the Church offers to others on the issue of abortion – based on a three-way discussion between Scripture, Tradition and Magisterium – is that abortion is morally wrong.

- The Catholic Church believes that God gives us the gift of life at the moment of conception ('Before I formed you in the womb I knew you; before you came to birth I consecrated you; I have appointed you as prophet to the nations'), and that from that moment every human being has the right to life.

- The unborn child is not simply part of the mother's body, even though it is completely dependent on the mother for sustaining its life. It is an individual with a separate identity.

- From conception onwards no one can interfere with that right – no mother, father or relative, no doctor or nurse, no parliament or law. As we have said above, all persons, not just some, have the right to life because of their nature – as persons. This includes unborn human beings.

- Catholics believe that we have the duty to provide love and care for all the people involved in this situation – the unborn child, the parents and the society. The Church believes that these three are the victims in any abortion, and so Catholic teaching on abortion will, in the long term, protect all three:

  The child (from death);

  Mum and Dad (from trauma, guilt, physical and mental illnesses, and spiritual damage);

  Society (from decline: disregard in any way for the dignity of human life, especially among the weakest and most vulnerable of society, will eventually lead to the corrosion of a community).

- Catholics realise that there are some very complex issues and situations surrounding abortion.

  The Church always thinks that adoption is a better solution than abortion in the case of an unwanted pregnancy.

  The Church never values one life more than the other, but always values the life of both mother and child. For example, if a pregnant mother needs some medical intervention to help save her life – say, chemotherapy for cancer or an anaesthetic after a heart attack – then the Church sees this as a moral course of action, even though it is might be that the treatment endangers the life of the unborn child.

This is called the *principle of double effect*: an action (an operation) will have two effects. The first effect is to save the mother's life, and is intended; while the second effect, not intended, may end the unborn life within her.

The Church recognises the tremendous pressures a pregnant woman may be under (e.g. from friends, relatives, personal and economic circumstances). The Church always looks to support in any way possible families, individuals, politicians and society, so that the justifications for abortion can be removed.

Other Christian Views on Human Life and Abortion

°   The Church of England / Anglicans share the Catholic view on the sanctity of human life. As a sister Christian community with a common creed, their understanding of the value of human life is almost identical to the Catholic approach, and the two Churches have worked together on many projects on behalf of the poor at home and abroad.

°   The Church of England recognises that there will be different views on the issue of abortion, but summarises its own position to be as follows: 'The Church of England combines strong opposition to abortion with a recognition that there can be – strictly limited – conditions under which it may be morally preferable to any available alternative.' It considers the number of abortions in the UK to be unacceptably high. **https://www. churchofengland.org/our-views/medical-ethics-health-social-care-policy/abortion.aspx**

°   As a series of broad considerations:

> It recognises the needs and wishes of the mother, especially in difficult circumstances (while not excluding the father in the decision-making process).

> It recognises what the law says: abortion is legal if there is a risk to the physical or mental health or life of the mother or a substantial risk of the child being born with physical or mental disabilities.

> It states its agreement with the general Catholic position of opposition to abortion as a great moral evil, seeing few exceptions in which the innocent should be deprived of life.

> One such exception is when the mother's life is threatened, though the termination of the pregnancy should be carried out as early as possible.

> There should be certainty that if a termination is carried out later than 24 weeks (this usually only happens when there is a threat to the mother or a serious disability in the child), the disability of the child should be such that the child would have survived only for a very short period of time.

> Adoption should be encouraged.

> Better sex education should be encouraged.

> Social injustice should be opposed, as this can lead to increased pressure to have abortions.

Discussion

Taking the considerations of either the Catholic or the Anglican Church as outlined above, put them in order of importance and compare your list with those of your colleagues.

Unit 1.7: Humanist Critiques Regarding the Sanctity of Life

In this unit we will explore some of the challenges to Catholic beliefs about the value of human life, looking specifically at humanism and Peter Singer's view on 'speciesism'.

Non-Religious World Views: humanists on the value of human life and on abortion

Here and Now: life here and now is the only life we get, according to humanists, and so they think that moral decisions should be based on what will allow us to live a full and happy life in this world.

Reason not Revelation: when making decisions about how to behave – ethical decisions – humanists, since they do not believe in God or gods, look to reason and human experience to help them.

Freedom not Faith: freedom, justice and happiness are highly valued as things which make the world a better place; the idea that God/gods might have the last word on such things is rejected.

Common Humanity: despite some differences at certain times in history and in certain places, humanists say that studies show that humans behave in pretty much the same way, especially when it comes to pursuing their basic needs and values, no matter what religious affiliation they profess.

Social Commitment: humanists claim to support any initiative which enables the individual to flourish, but which also promotes the well-being of society and allows human beings to live together in a cooperative manner.

Although there is no 'official humanist' position on abortion, humanists tend towards the pro-choice position. They think that abortion is morally acceptable as a personal choice.

° Humanists support the legalisation of abortion so that unsafe, or 'back-street', abortions, do not take place.

° Humanists do not consider life 'sacred' but they have respect for human life. They think that, rather than 'sanctity of life', the 'quality of life' of mother, unborn, or both is much more useful in helping us decide what to do, especially if there is a conflict of interests.

° Humanists do not think a foetus becomes a person with feelings and rights until 'well after conception'.

KEY TERMS

Humanism = an approach which excludes notions of God and eternity from moral decisions.

Speciesism = according more importance to one species than to other life forms.

Utilitarianism = a measure of morality based on levels of happiness.

- While acknowledging that it is a complex situation with lots of factors, humanists think that preference should be given to a more mature human being who already exists in the world. Effectively this supports the woman's right to choose.

- A final decision must be carefully thought through, considering both short-term and long-term possible effects. For this reason, adoption should be considered, as well as whether the mother/parents have the ability to care for an ill or disabled child, and the quality of life that could be offered to the child.

- Humanists do not usually think that abortion is the best way of making sure that every child is a wanted child. They believe that what would help reduce the number of abortions would be better sex education and more access to contraception.

Peter Singer on the Value of Human Life and on Abortion

A humanist who would be critical of the Catholic view of the value of human life would be the Australian philosopher Peter Singer (b. 1946). Singer believes that we should help as many people as possible to enjoy life and eliminate the suffering of as many people as possible – that is, we should increase the pleasure and decrease the suffering of 'humanity'. This is a form of utilitarianism.

Singer rejects the notion of 'sanctity of life', preferring instead the idea of 'quality of life'. Quality of life is more important when we are deciding what is right and wrong. He says that quality of life for all animal species (including humans) is related to the amount of suffering/enjoyment (or pleasure) they have – those who suffer more have a worse quality of life, and those who enjoy more have a better quality of life.

Based on this, Singer believes that it is okay to kill some human beings, as it will reduce the suffering and so increase the overall 'enjoyment' of 'humanity' in the world. When working out what is right and wrong, we must put aside irrational factors such as feelings and emotions, and base our decisions on cool, critical thinking.

On the abortion issue, Singer agrees with Catholics that embryos are human beings from the moment of conception. But he disagrees that they are 'persons'.

Singer makes a distinction between human beings who are biologically human beings (which he says is undeniable, from the moment of conception), and human beings who are also persons. Only a human being who is a 'rational and self-conscious being' (*Practical Ethics*, Cambridge: Cambridge University Press, 1993, p. 87) is a person.

Any other type of human being is a 'non-person human' – that is, a biological member of our species, but unable to think, feel, hope and choose. Singer believes that foetuses, new-born babies and elderly people with dementia fit into this category of non-person human. And so it is okay to kill them, if that death reduces the overall suffering of humanity.

Singer would also be very critical of the Catholic position that human life possesses a unique value compared with the life of other species. Anthropocentrism (making human beings central), a making of distinctions between different species and human beings, and treating animals less favourably than human beings is, in Singer's opinion, discriminatory against animals – that is, it is 'speciesist'.

Animals show similar responses to human beings to certain experiences – they can know, for example, both pain and pleasure – and so they have interests which must be taken into account. Just as people of both sexes and all races should have their interests taken into account when ethical decisions are being taken, so too animals should not be discounted when we make ethical decisions.

Speciesism is morally wrong and we should give the same respect to an animal that we give to a human being of the same mental capacity. So, a conscious dog or cat that can suffer has more mental capacity, and is more of a person, than a human without consciousness such as an unborn or an infant baby.

Catholic Responses to these Critiques

1   First, Catholics would respond to Singer by saying that the amount of suffering and pleasure of 'humanity' in the world is not something that can be worked out using 'sums'. If I reduce the suffering of one person, it does not follow that I have reduced the overall amount of suffering of 'humanity' in the world.

Other Christians would agree. C. S. Lewis says that if one person is suffering toothache of intensity X, and another person in the same room is suffering toothache of intensity X, there might be 2X amount of pain in the room, but nobody in the room is suffering 2X. The 'overall suffering of humanity' is not something that can be added to or subtracted from, because no one actually suffers all that suffering.

2   Second, Catholics would say that human beings, because of their soul, are and remain persons, whether enjoying life or suffering in life, conscious or unconscious. A human being is still a person with dignity when unborn, asleep or in a coma. It is not consciousness or awareness that makes a human being a human being.

Singer himself confronted this critique in his own life when his mother began to suffer severely from Alzheimer's disease. His reaction was intriguing – far from disregarding her state, he proved to be a very considerate son, looking after her generously while 'admitting' that as a philosopher he was acting 'unethically'!

3   Third, Catholics would be critical of the artificial division of a human being into cool, critical, rational intelligence and irrational emotions when making moral decisions. Reason and emotions work together when we make decisions about right and wrong. It is the heart, not the mind, that fills with deep joy when we fall in love; but we do not park our common sense at the door, especially if we have been in love before!

For example, when choosing our marriage partner, the wonderful emotions of romance, being in love and fancying someone have to be balanced with the practical, nitty-gritty issues such as how well we get on, how often we fight, what his/her family is like, where we will live, how we will support ourselves, and so on. One without the other is a recipe for disaster! The heart, the gut, the instinct, intuition and rational intelligence all come into play when we make decisions about how to behave.

4   Fourth, with regard to the critique of speciesism, Catholics would say that human beings should indeed respect and care for animals, and not act cruelly towards them. Animals are God's creatures, part of his plan and giving glory to him because of their existence (CCC 2416). And so human beings do something unworthy of human dignity when they behave cruelly towards other species (CCC 2418).

At the same time, however, Catholics believe that only human beings are made in God's image and so only they have this special dignity (CCC 2417). Human beings are to love animals, but not in the way that they should love human beings (CCC 2418). Animals can be used for food, clothing, leisure and work. They can also be used in experimentation if this is done morally and within acceptable limits and if it contributes to caring for or saving human life (CCC 2417).

5   Fifth, while it is easy to see the links between chimpanzees and the human species, it is not so easy to see the links between human beings and a bluebottle or other insects. Are we really to be accused of speciesism for destroying a wasp's nest?

Does this also reveal a contradiction between Singer's charge of speciesism and the fact that he says personhood and quality of life are measured by consciousness? If a dog or cat is judged a person because of its consciousness, is this not a judgement by human standards? The more like a human they are, the more dignity they have and the better we should treat them morally? But is that not also anthropocentric?

Discussion

While Catholics disagree with humanists' stance on abortion, it is essential to realise that they can agree with humanists on many of their core values, not least because Catholics understand Jesus to be the exemplary human/ist! The following are values they can agree on:
- the importance of this life –
  I came that you might have life, and life to the full
- the importance of reason –
  You must love the Lord with all your mind...
- the importance of freedom –
  If the Son shall make you free, you shall be free indeed
- the importance of our common humanity –
  Do unto others as you would have done to you
- the importance of social commitment –
  What you do to the least of my brothers, you do to me

Can you find any other common ground between Catholics and humanists?

Unit 1.8a: Where Did the Bible Come From? The origins, structure and literary forms of Scripture

CORE IDEA

Here we look more closely at the origins, structure and main types of writing in Scripture (the Bible), which Catholics understand to be an inspired library which reveals the Word of God. and Peter Singer's view on 'speciesism'.

The Bible: oral tradition (based on events), written tradition and editing (putting together)

So far our focus in the course has involved mega-questions such as why is there a universe, the religious and non-religious dimensions of evolution, and, in the last unit, whether wasps have the same rights as us! This section might appear to have a narrower focus, but as we shall see, studying the Bible in more detail will open up a new world of understanding about life, the universe and everything!

What we now have as the Bible is the outcome of a process which took about 2,000 years to complete and which involved three phases – speaking, writing and collecting.

- **Speaking:** the oral tradition: unlike now, back in the day, no one could write. As God was revealed to the Chosen People of Israel, oral accounts were passed on first by those who experienced the events first hand, and then by successive generations. There was no other way – talking was humanity's original version of telecoms!

- **Writing:** the scrolls of Scripture: unlike you, back in the day, no one could read! Beginning around 1000 BC, scribes in Israel began to write down parts of the oral traditions about important people and events – Abraham, Moses, the Kings, the Prophets – indeed, all the joys and tragedies of the Chosen People. Much later, the Gospels of Jesus also had to be written down as the eye witnesses died out. Likewise, the letters of Paul and Peter were composed in response to the needs of the Early Church.

- **Collecting:** the Bible as a library: unlike now, back in the day, there was no Bible! All these holy writings were to be found on separate scrolls – if you asked where the Scriptures were, they would point to a cupboard! It wasn't until humans got better at making paper that eventually the writings could be collected into a single codex (an ancient book), and by then there were arguments as to which should be in and which should be left out. After much discussion, the 'canon' or 'standard list' of Scriptures was eventually defined by Pope Damasus in AD 382, and this remains the collection Catholics refer to as the Bible today (see 'The Canon of the Catholic Bible' on the next page).

KEY TERMS

Scripture = the inspired collection of writings called the Bible.

Inspired = 'God-breathed' – the influence of the Holy Spirit on the people who wrote the Scriptures. (In this sense we can speak of God as being the ultimate 'author' of Scripture.)

Old Testament = writings about God and humanity understood principally through the people of Israel.

New Testament = writings about God and humanity understood through Jesus and the early Church.

IN DETAIL

The Bible: a library of books divided into two testaments

° The Bible is like a library of several books (in the Catholic Canon, there are 46 in the Old Testament and 27 in the New Testament = 73 in total). Any library is a rich and complex collection, and so the Church seeks to interpret the Bible to help us understand it better.

° The first way it does this is by dividing the Bible into the two sections shown above: the Old Testament (sometimes called the Hebrew/Jewish Scriptures) and the New Testament (sometimes called the Christian Scriptures). Testament is a word which means 'covenant', or 'agreement' between two parties.

The Old Testament, dealing with the creation of the universe and human beings, tells of God's 'deal' with all of humanity, but especially with the people of Israel. God wanted to use Israel as 'a light to the nations', a kind of magnet to draw all other people to know Him. Most of the Old Testament recounts the ups and downs of God's dealings with Israel.

The New Testament, starting with the Gospel (four versions) of Jesus' life, tells of God's new covenant with all people through his Son, Jesus. It tells the story of how the God of love relates to us all in his Son and how his followers, the Church, handed on the Gospel, or good news, of God's self-revelation in Jesus. It shows how they tried to embody this Gospel of love in their lives. It also contains some of the letters written by some of the apostles and other Christian leaders.

Canon = an ancient word meaning ruler/measuring stick/standard/guide – nothing to do with explosives!

Canon of Scripture = the accepted standard list of the books that make up the Bible.

Literary forms = Different writings found in Scripture such as law, history, prophecy, letters and parables.

Aetiology = ancient writings which explain the origins of things with symbols, images and imagination.

THE CANON OF THE CATHOLIC BIBLE

HEBREW SCRIPTURES THE OLD TESTAMENT	CHRISTIAN SCRIPTURES THE NEW TESTAMENT

THE PENTATEUCH	WISDOM BOOKS	GOSPELS	NON-PAULINE LETTERS
GENESIS	JOB	MATTHEW	HEBREWS
EXODUS	PSALMS	MARK	JAMES
LEVITICUS	PROVERBS	LUKE	1 PETER
NUMBERS	ECCLESIASTES	JOHN	2 PETER
DEUTERONOMY	SONG OF SOLOMON		1 JOHN
	WISDOM	**HISTORICAL**	2 JOHN
HISTORICAL BOOKS	SIRACH	ACTS OF THE APOSTLES	3 JOHN
			JUDE
JOSHUA JUDITH	THE PROPHETS	**LETTERS OF PAUL**	
JUDGES ESTHER			**APOCALYPTIC**
RUTH 1 MACCABEES	ISAIAH JONAH	ROMANS 2 TIMOTHY	
1 SAMUEL 2 MACCABEES	JEREMIAH MICAH	1 CORINTHIANS TITUS	REVELATION
2 SAMUEL	LAMENTATIONS NAHUM	2 CORINTHIANS PHILEMON	
1 KINGS	BARUCH HABAKKUK	GALATIANS	
2 KINGS	EZEKIEL ZEPHANIAH	EPHESIANS	
1 CHRONICLES	DANIEL HAGGAI	PHILIPPIANS	
2 CHRONICLES	HOSEA ZECHARIAH	COLOSSIANS	
EZRA	JOEL MALACHI	1 THESSALONIANS	
NEHEMIAH	AMOS	2 THESSALONIANS	
TOBIT	OBADIAH	1 TIMOTHY	

LITERARY FORMS IN THE BIBLE

Introduction

- Every day we experience different forms of written communication – questions, text messages, announcements, jokes, readings, stories, lessons, etc. – and we know that some types of writing are harder to understand than others. This is even more the case when we are reading poems and plays from previous times, like Shakespeare, when we may need the teacher to help us so we don't get the wrong end of the stick.

- This is also true of the Bible, which has lots of different types of literature – the Church says: 'In order to discover the sacred authors' intention, the reader must take into account the conditions of their time and culture, the literary genres in use at that time, and the modes of feeling, speaking and narrating then current' (CCC 110)

- Another name for literary genres is literary forms, which means different types of writing. Because the Bible is a library of 73 books, we need to bear in mind that we could be dealing with several different literary forms as we move from book to book – it is like moving from the chemistry section to the poetry section of a library, or reading the football reports after the business section of a newspaper. Below are some of the more common types of writing in the Bible.

Old Testament

- **Law:** writings which offer instructions on how to live – e.g. the Ten Commandments. The first five books (the Pentateuch) of the Bible are full of this sort of writing, and so collectively they are called The Law (Torah in Hebrew).

- **Stories of Origins:** in some parts we also find creation meditations, like Genesis 1, and symbolic narratives, such as Genesis 2–3. For example, a flashy word for the Adam and Eve story is aetiology – a kind of parable which explains in a symbolic way 'why things are as they are'.

- **History:** those books of the Old Testament which narrate the story of God's people from the time they entered the Promised Land (1200 BC). They encourage Israel to imitate the great heroes of their past by doing what God asks – keeping the 'deal', the covenant.

- **Prophecy:** prophecy means 'to speak on behalf of'. The prophets spoke for God to his people in the present moment, challenging them and their leaders to keep the deal with God. The prophets spoke of Israel as being the future light for all the nations, and of having a Messiah who would attract all peoples to God.

- **Wisdom:** through good times and bad, these writings are prayers, sayings, songs, love poetry, philosophical reflections on life, and advice on how to live.

New Testament

- **Gospels:** proclamations of the 'good news' (= 'gospel') about the love of God made visible in Jesus, who is God among us.

- **Historical (Acts of the Apostles):** an account of the spread of the Gospel in the Early Church, particularly through the experiences of Peter and Paul.

- **Letters:** actual letters sent by early Christian leaders such as Peter, Paul and John to Christian communities, encouraging them, guiding them and addressing specific issues in the Early Church.

- **Apocalyptic:** a richly symbolic way of writing designed to encourage and strengthen the Early Church through the message that God is in charge of history and will remain faithful.

Discussion

What different types of writing have you read in the past week? What is your favourite type of writing, and why? What type of writing stays in your memory best? Why do some types of writing have to be composed in a certain way and others differently?

The Bible is best understood as 'an inspired library', but why do you think the Church took time to agree what writings should go into the official collection, or canon? Why do you think some people give the impression that the Bible dropped out of the sky?

Unit 1.8b: Biblical Inspiration, Revelation and How Catholics Interpret Scripture

CORE IDEA

We will explore what Catholics mean by 'inspiration' and 'revelation' and the typically Catholic way of understanding the Bible.

Biblical Inspiration and Revelation

The Second Letter to Timothy says: 'All scripture is inspired by God and can profitably be used for teaching, for refuting error, for guiding people's lives and teaching them to be holy' (2 Timothy 3:16). So what do Catholics actually mean when they say that 'the Bible is inspired by the Holy Spirit', or that 'God is the Author of Scripture', or that 'the Bible is the Word of God', 'God's Word in human words'?

First, and most obviously, they do not mean that God appeared with a pen in his hand and wrote on a scroll, nor that he whispered into the ear of a Jewish or early Christian PA, who then faithfully wrote down everything that was said!

Catholics believe that the Bible emerged from certain events, which were interpreted and passed on in oral traditions, before eventually being written down by human authors in different literary forms.

Inspiration means, therefore, that God's Holy Spirit influenced the story of the Chosen People, helping them to perceive and understand certain things about God and human beings, at every stage of their history.

In certain events, God was especially present and revealed his purpose through those events (e.g. Exodus 3:1–15), and those who understood passed on these oral traditions and others were inspired to write them down.

Lastly, those members of the Church who were involved in the process of the Scriptures being gathered, selected and edited into the canon of Scripture are also considered to have been inspired.

In other words, because the process was inspired, Catholics believe that the Bible contains God's revelation. Revelation means 'uncovering' or 'showing'. Here it means that in the Bible God communicates himself and his will to human beings. God shows, using the Bible, that he is Love, and that out of that love he creates all people and wishes for them to be saved. In order to explore this more fully, the Catholic Church teaches that we need to know how to read the Bible.

Two Ways of Reading the Bible: fundamentalist (literalist) and Catholic

Remember that understanding the Bible is not simply a matter of reading it. It is sometimes difficult to understand what the authors

KEY TERMS

Inspired = 'God-breathed' – the Holy Spirit working through human beings.

Revelation = God's self-communication to human beings.

Fundamentalist = someone who tends to read all the different books of the Bible in the same literal way.

of the Scriptures were trying to communicate: 'In order to discover the sacred authors' intention, the reader must take into account the conditions of their time and culture, the literary genres in use at that time, and the modes of feeling, speaking and narrating then current' (CCC 110).

° Some Christian groups disagree with this. They believe that in order to understand the Bible, all we have to do is read it, because the meaning of what we are reading is obvious and self-evident. These Christians take every word and event mentioned in the Bible as a straightforward, literal description of what the author is trying to say. This way of reading the Bible is called a literalist approach to reading the Bible, and is often associated with groups of Christians who are called Christian fundamentalists.

° Catholics believe, however (in common with certain other Christian groups), that if we are to understand more fully what God wants to reveal to us in the Bible, we have to read the Bible in context – that is to say, in the context in which it was written by the author. This approach says that we have to take into account certain things like literary form, and the beliefs held by the author and his generation.

° The fundamentalist reads every passage in the same way, but this does a disservice to the nature of the Bible. If we cannot recognise different literary forms, we will not understand the message that a book is trying to communicate. Similarly, Catholics says that if we do not know the difference between law, history, wisdom, prophecy, myth, parable, allegory, debate, poem, legend, letter and apocalyptic writing, then we will fail to understand much of what the Bible is saying and what God is trying to reveal.

° Another important consideration when trying to understand the Bible's authors is the need to 'take into account the conditions of their time and culture … and the modes of feeling, speaking and narrating then current' (CCC 110). The authors were writing in the context of their own setting and time, with all the customs, beliefs, limits, strengths and weaknesses that this involved. A biblical author alive 2,000–2,500 years ago would have shared the assumptions and opinions of the other people of the time about many things – for example, that the world was flat and not round, or (for much of Israelite history) that God only loved Israel, the 'Chosen People'.

° To say that the author is inspired is to say that he has had certain truthful insights about God and our relationship with God. We are not claiming that everything else he writes is 100% true or that he knew about things (such as chemistry, physics, geography, biology, psychology) that nobody else in his country or generation knew. The inspiration does not extend to the other opinions and assumptions of the author. Just because his theology is cutting edge, it doesn't automatically follow that his science is bang up to date!

Discussion

Joseph Campbell studied the cultures of the world, and one of the conclusions he came to was that 'the Greatest Stories are always True!' What do you think he meant by that? Can stories teach us truths? Are there truths in *Lord of the Rings*, *Star Wars* and the *Harry Potter* stories that are relevant to our lives? Can a parable like the Good Samaritan help us become a better person? If so, why? Does it matter how many thieves there were or whether it happened on a Tuesday or a Thursday? For it to be 'true', does it matter if it happened at all?

Unit 1.10: What the Two Creation Accounts Tell Us about God

CORE IDEA

In this unit we explore the Catholic understanding of the nature of God as portrayed in the two creation accounts of Genesis 1 and 2 – as creator, eternal, transcendent, omnipotent, benevolent and ineffable.

As we have seen, Catholics understand the Scriptures to be a library of 73 books containing several types of writing. Genesis 1–2, the two creation stories, were penned out of a deep sense of wonder at why things are as they are. There is enormous potential for confusion when people make the category mistake of reading Genesis 1–2 as history or science.

What does Genesis 1:1 – 2:4a tell us about God?

¹In the beginning God created the heavens and the earth. ²Now the earth was a formless void, there was darkness over the deep, and God's spirit hovered over the water. ³God said, 'Let there be light', and there was light. (Genesis 1:1–3)

- Only God is eternal. Genesis 1:1: 'In the beginning God…' – only God has no beginning. God is the ultimate reality, the One who is, Being itself, without beginning or end. The Hebrew text doesn't use the word 'make' – it uses the word for 'create'.

- God is omnipotent (all-powerful). The difference between nothing and something is infinite, so creation must require infinite power. God is the eternal and infinite one, the Being who has neither beginning nor end, so he must also be the omnipotent one, creating *ex nihilo*.

- Creation happens at God's word. 1:3 'God said, "Let there be light", and there was light' – God speaks creation into existence. For Christians, the universe is not a random accident, a cosmic coincidence that just happens to be here, nor has it always been here.

- God is transcendent (beyond all that exists). Unlike the many pagan gods and goddesses who make the universe out of pre-existing 'stuff', the omnipotent God is not one god among many, not one being among many, not one powerful thing or reality among many. Rather, God is the Supreme Reality, beyond all that exists, the source of all that exists, but not in any way confined by it. That is to say, God is transcendent.

KEY TERMS

Genesis = the first Book of the Bible, pondering creation, human beings, sin and covenant.

God as eternal = without beginning or end.

God as Creator = 'maker of all things visible and invisible'.

Ex nihilo = Latin, meaning 'out of nothing'.

God as omnipotent = all-powerful.

God as transcendent = God is beyond our reality, beyond time and space.

- God is ineffable (beyond description). We cannot begin to imagine or describe what God is like, for God goes beyond/transcends/surpasses any of our thoughts, images and words about him. We can and must try to talk of God, but our words, our images and our thoughts are never up the task. That is to say, God is ineffable.

- God is omnibenevolent (all-loving). God is infinitely loving and infinitely generous. He is the Supreme Being who needs nothing and so cannot be self-interested, and yet he created the universe with us in it. So Creation is the result of God's love. Creation comes into existence out of God's infinite love. It is 'God-loved' into being.

What does Genesis 2:4b–24 tells us about God?

The second Creation story shares some themes in common with the first, but there are also some interesting and important 'tweaks'.

- God as Creator? In Genesis 2:4b we are told that God made the earth and the heavens. In Genesis 2:7 we are told that God formed Man from the dust of the earth and breathed life into him through his nostrils. Later (Genesis 2:18–23), so that Man (Adam) would not be alone, God makes all the animals and birds. But none is suitable, and so God forms Woman (Eve) from Man's rib. These verses seem to confirm the notion of God as Origin, Source, or Creator of everything, including human beings.

- God as omnipotent? Being Creator would seem to confirm God's omnipotence but there is a sense in which God shares his creative power. There is no one to till the earth and God seeks help in looking after the garden (2:15) so at the very least we can say humanity has a role to play in God's creation.

- God as transcendent AND immanent? Well, as we said above, if God created out of nothing, he has to be omnipotent, and therefore unlimited and transcendent. But this second story emphasises something else – God's immanence. That is to say, God is involved with his creation, especially with humans in their day-to-day lives. We see that he formed Man from the dust – God 'gets his hands dirty' in creation. God is omnipresent, everywhere, here and now, with his human creation.

- God as omnibenevolent? Yes. God is concerned about Man's loneliness and provides other species to keep him company, and then finally Woman, so that they can become 'one flesh' – Adam recognises Eve as 'bone from my bones, and flesh from my flesh' (Genesis 2:23–24).

Although the second Creation account tells us of God's omnipotence and other qualities, it is less cosmic and more anthropocentric (focused on human beings), underlining God's closeness to us and his desire to be in relationship with us. Because it is an aetiology, it is a story about human beings and their place in creation and in relationship to the Creator God.

Taking the Creation Accounts Together

If the creation accounts are taken together, the author is (or authors are) trying to communicate the revelation from God that all of creation, all that exists, is not simply 'there' – it is contingent and has been brought into being by the infinite love and generosity of a necessary, omnipotent, transcendent, immanent, omnibenevolent God. The cosmos is, ultimately, and despite all indications to the contrary, a friendly place, because all reality is God-shaped!

Discussion

Word Power Part 1

- We take for granted all the forms of communication we have and all the ways we can keep records. What are some of the issues regarding traditions passed on by word of mouth? Why were there so few scrolls/books in the ancient world? How did those who wrote them make sure they were accurate? Hebrew was written without vowels – like TXT MSGS. What problems could arise from that?

- The prophets transformed the world with words; just like God in Genesis 1, their words bring light to darkness. Can you think of any examples of people in our own day who have changed the world by their inspired words?

CORE IDEA

Human beings as Imago Dei – 'the image of God'. In this unit we explore what the Genesis creation accounts teach us about human dignity, free will, stewardship of creation and the sanctity of life.

Genesis 1 – 2:4a and 2:4b–24: a closer look at human beings

In the last unit we looked at what the Catholic reading of the creation stories tells us about God. Now we will look at what the Catholic reading tells us about human beings.

In Genesis 1 – 2:4a we see:

- *Imago Dei.* Genesis 1:27 says: 'God created man in the image of himself, in the image of God he created him, male and female he created them.' Human beings, male and female, are made last in creation, and are made in the *imago Dei*, in the image of God – they reflect something of God in creation.

- **Human dignity and sanctity of life.** This gives humans a special status and sanctity in creation. We reflect something of God in our intelligence, our free will and our ability to relate and love. This is because our very being belongs to God, so our lives have holiness, or sanctity.

- **Male and female he created them.** A traditional understanding of this text is that God is imaged in mutual love. This will be taken further in the understanding of God as Trinity as revealed in Christianity.

- **Freedom to flourish.** Encouraged by God to flourish and multiply (Genesis 1:28), human beings are invited to use their free will to be co-creators with God, becoming involved in the procreation of human offspring.

- **Goodness of Creation.** Again and again, at the end of each of the six days of Creation, God declares what was created that day to be 'good'. All that is brought into being by the omnibenevolent, generous and living God is good.

- **Light of reason.** We saw in Unit 1.2 that Creation happened at God's word. 'God said, "Let there be light", and there was light' (Genesis 1:3). This means that the existence of the whole universe and all that is to be found in it is not simply 'just there', but rather 'intelligently there'. This means it can be understood by minds that explore it as humans do through science and other fields of knowledge.

KEY TERMS

Imago Dei = Latin for 'the image of God'.

Free will = humans can decide their own actions.

Stewardship = humans caring for the creation.

Dignity = humans are worthy of respect.

Sanctity of life = human life belongs to God and is therefore sacred.

Creation of Eve by Andrea Pisano, Florence, Italy.
Zvonimir Atletic / Shutterstock.com

- **Human stewardship.** In Genesis 1:26–29 God gives human beings a special mastery/dominion over the other species, as well as over the plants for food. Catholics believe that being made in the image of God, humans are also stewards of creation, exercising a special responsibility for its care. As Pope Francis pointed out in his 2015 encyclical letter *Laudato Si'*, human beings must regard all creatures as part of one created family, since they share one and the same Father in God the Creator.

In Genesis 2:4b–24 we see:

- **The *imago Dei*.** God creates Man, Adam, from the soil (Genesis 2:7). Human and humility both come from the same Latin word, humus, meaning 'soil' or 'earth'. Adam is materially made of the earth but at the same time has the divine breath of God, the spark of life, a soul.

- **Human dignity and sanctity of life.** This soul/principle of life belongs to God alone and distinguishes human life as sacred.

- **Male and female.** In this second creation story God takes his time bringing together Male and Female. Far from being an afterthought, the creation of Eve demonstrates our need for one another and is the highlight of the account, drawing a love song/rap out of Adam (Genesis 2:23).

- **Freedom to flourish.** God places the tree of the knowledge of good and evil in the garden (Genesis 2:9). In 2:16–17, Man is invited to use the freedom to do God's will. We also see in 2:18–24 the cooperation of man and woman, their complementarity.

- **Goodness of creation.** Man is placed in Eden (Genesis 2:8–9), an idyllic place full of goodness, to live life and enjoy the goodness of God's gifts in creation.

- **Light of reason.** Working with God, Man is invited to name the animals (Genesis 2:20). This can be read as an invitation to explore the creation scientifically. *Kata logon* means 'according to the word': Adam names the animals and chooses between them, according to the differences placed in them by God's creative word.

- **Human stewardship.** Human beings are granted the gift of rationality in order to share in God's intelligent love for creation, to order, 'cultivate and take care of it' (Genesis 2:16). We are told in 2:5 that there was no bush or plant, and no man to care for the earth. God invites humans to work with him in caring for creation.

> Human beings are both earthly and divine, material and spiritual, of this world and the next, temporal and eternal (2:7). Or, as Shakespeare puts it: 'How infinite in faculty … this quintessence of dust'.
>
> *Hamlet, Act II, Scene 2*

Taking the Creation Accounts Together

- **Creation is a sign of God's love.** Creation, therefore is good. Since God is the Supreme Being, Supreme Reality, and does not need the world, the existence of creation is a sign that everything has been loved into being by God's loving, generous omnibenevolence.

- **Image of God.** Human beings are made in the *imago Dei*. We are one reality in two dimensions, body and soul: 'it is because of its spiritual soul that the body made of matter becomes a living, human body; spirit and matter, in man … their union forms a single nature' (CCC 365).

- **Sanctity of life.** All human life belongs to God alone, the Creator, the Giver of life, and so is sacred, from conception to natural death. Relationship with God is not an 'extra' to human life – something we do on a Sunday, if at all – if God creates human existence, and if the principle of life belongs to God.

- **Stewards of creation.** Since all creatures are created by God, all creatures are connected to one another and can be understood as a Creation family. This is why Saint Francis of Assisi refers to his 'Brother Sun' and 'Sister Moon'. Intelligent and free human beings – made in the image of God – have a special status as stewards of Creation. With status comes responsibility. The world is not just about us!

- **Freedom.** But we cannot exercise responsible mastery over others unless we first of all know how to master ourselves! *I am responsible for the gift of myself too.* 'The mastery over the world that God offered man from the beginning was realised above all within man himself: mastery of self' (CCC 377). The human tragedy of losing freedom is most obvious when appetites get the better of someone through addiction, leading to broken health, broken hearts and broken lives.

- **Relationship.** Relationship helps to complete human beings, who are incomplete if they do not relate to others in love and walk with them through life.

Discussion

Word Power Part 2

In Genesis 2, the parable has God do a mysterious thing. He makes the little groundling fall into a deep death-like sleep and takes out one of his ribs and encloses it in flesh (Genesis 2:21). Symbolically this divides the original cloddy humanoid into two sections, or sexes. It is then love at first sight when God brings the 'new' groundling to the reawakened Adam, who is so delighted that he breaks into Hebrew rap:

'This at last is bone from my bones, and flesh from my flesh! This is to be called woman, for this was taken from man.'

Genesis 2:23

OK, so maybe the rap isn't brilliant and you could perhaps do better for your Valentine – but it is very significant that the first words exchanged in the Bible are a love song. Does this mean it is the desire for relationship which makes us communicate, because on our own we are incomplete (see Genesis 2:24)? Notice that when we sulk or are frightened we say nothing, but when we are with friends we can't stop talking. We can sometimes be cruel to our friends by NOT talking to them. Is it possible then to imagine a world without words? Is there a sense in which we are created by words? Discuss!

: A Comparison of Catholics' and Humanists' Views on Preserving the Planet and the Environment

CORE IDEA

In this unit we explore the Catholic understanding of the nature of God as portrayed in the two creation accounts of Genesis 1 and 2 – as creator, eternal, transcendent, omnipotent, benevolent and ineffable.

INTRODUCTION

∘ Catholics see human beings as stewards (Genesis 1:26–29), not parasites or exploiters of Creation. This is arguably our first religious duty: 'Yahweh God took the man and settled him in the garden of Eden to cultivate and take care of it' (Genesis 2:15). Part of our stewardship involves taking care of the planet and the environment, which will be here long after we have left, and which need to be protected for future generations.

∘ The Seventh Commandment is: 'You shall not steal' (Exodus 20:15). Catholics believe that this 'requires respect for the universal destination of goods' (CCC 2401). The goods of the earth, including a healthy environment and an inhabitable planet, are God's gift to all people, including those not yet born. A refusal to preserve the planet and keep it safe is theft.

∘ Humanists do not look to God/gods or the supernatural in order to understand how the universe works. They say that we should base the way we behave on natural empathy and a concern for human beings and other animals. Since they do not believe in either a life beyond this one or any discernible overall purpose to the universe, they believe that human beings have to give meaning to their lives here and now by seeking happiness and helping others to do the same.

Similarities and Differences

Despite the very basic and obvious differences between humanists and Catholics, it would be incorrect to say that they share nothing in common. There is plenty of overlap, and there are some differences:

∘ Catholics and humanists both view human beings as having a unique importance (because of their intelligence) in preserving the planet and the environment – but Catholics see this intelligence as grounded in the image of God in each person.

∘ Catholics and humanists agree on the importance of science and free intellectual enquiry in enabling us to understand how the universe works and discover more sustainable ways of living on

KEY TERMS

Laudato Si' = a letter by Pope Francis in 2015 about our responsibility for the environment.

Universal destination of goods = things that belong to everyone and to future generations.

the planet – but Catholics believe that science 'works' because there is a God-given intelligibility stamped into creation by the mind/intelligence of the Creator.

- Catholics and humanists both believe that humans are free and must use this freedom responsibly to safeguard the future of the planet – but Catholics see this freedom as part of the God-given dignity of human beings, and believe that wisdom from God can help us do this better.

- Catholics and humanists both believe that human beings should be happy and flourish – but Catholics say that this is because true happiness involves knowing God's will for us, and that the only way that this can happen is by living life in the way God intended, which is revealed in Jesus as love. Christianity is the real and radical humanism. Catholics are Christian humanists.

- Catholics and humanists both believe that the planet and the environment should be cared for by human beings. The Catholic justification for this is because the world is part of God's gift of creation, and so must be preserved so that people today and in future generations can flourish and come to know, love and serve God by loving one another.

Perhaps the main differences relate to reproduction and 'speciesism':

- Catholics and other Christians would emphasise that humans are called to flourish and multiply. Humans are radically different from animals and their interests must come first.

- Humanists support birth-control programmes because they see over-population as a threat to preserving the planet and future happiness. Likewise, humanists are increasingly recognising the rights of animals over those of humans in order to avoid the accusation of 'speciesism' associated with thinkers like Peter Singer.

Discussion

'The social environment has suffered damage. This is ultimately due to the same evil: the notion that there are no indisputable truths to guide our lives, and hence human freedom is limitless. We have forgotten that "man is not only a freedom which he creates for himself. Man does not create himself. He is spirit and will, but also nature"' (Pope Francis, *Laudato Si'* #6). How far does this support the view that 'Catholics are Christian humanists'? What lies behind this statement, and do you agree with it?

Unit 1.13: Catholic Understanding of Creation Expressed in Art

CORE IDEA

Catholic understanding of eternal truths about creation, God and human beings, expressed in Michelangelo's *The Creation of Adam* (Sistine Chapel, Vatican City).

Art: the eternal in time?

As well as being a world-famous writer, G. K. Chesterton was a decent artist, having studied at art school. He said, 'All art is born when the temporary touches the eternal', when Earth touches Heaven, when the physical and the spiritual meet.

Genesis tells us that Adam was both temporary and eternal, physical and spiritual – he was made from the earth, but had the breath of God in him. What Chesterton meant is that art is an attempt to express the eternal in the here and now, the meaning of life in this temporary and passing world. Painting, sculpture, literature, music, dance, films, etc. are an attempt by human beings living in this world to express something of the meaning of life, God's plan, God's truth, something from beyond this world. The artist senses that the cosmos is absolutely rammed full of mystery and meaning, and tries to communicate something of that fullness, however imperfectly. In a sense the artist will always be trying to express something that cannot be fully expressed.

One artist who spent his whole life trying to do this was Michelangelo Buonarroti (1475–1564).

'The Creation of Adam', by Michelangelo

This work of Michelangelo is found on the ceiling of the Sistine Chapel in the Vatican (the chapel in which popes are elected to lead the Catholic Church). It is called The Creation of Adam, and it is the most famous of the nine scenes taken from the Book of Genesis which decorate the ceiling.

KEY TERMS

Michelangelo = Italian artist who lived between 1475 and 1564.

Sistine Chapel = a little chapel within the Vatican City.

omnipotent = all-powerful.

imago Dei = Latin for 'image of God'.

Discussion

Discuss quickly with your neighbour which eternal truths Michelangelo was trying to express through his art in The Creation of Adam.

Analysis

- God (on the right) is the omnipotent Creator, a dynamic presence in the universe, full of energy and vitality, moving through the clouds amid a group of angelic creatures; we human beings (represented by Adam on the left) are the sleepy, laid-back, earth-bound creatures being called into existence by God. Adam is emerging from the soil/earth from which Genesis 2:7 says God fashioned him.

- God is the eternal one, bearded and much older than the young man Adam: the relationship is one of Father–child. So we are all God's children, sharing the same Father, made one family by being brought into existence by the same Creator God. This idea of a heavenly parent is pushed further by the red background behind God, which is possibly an image for God's womb, and the green ribbon hanging loose, perhaps a symbol of the umbilical cord, which was cut loose by God in giving birth to us. We are his children, but in creating us with free will, he sets us free.

- God loves us first: God is proactive, and his index finger is full of tension and energy as he reaches out to touch Adam's finger. Adam, by contrast, moves only a little, barely meeting God halfway. Perhaps this represents our spiritual sluggishness and our inability to do what God asks without God's help (grace).

- God is life-giver: the touch of God represents the spark of life being given to us, the soul being placed in us. Life is the gift of God and belongs to God alone. Life is sacred. Fingertip to fingertip, Michelangelo tells the world of the sanctity of human life.

- *Imago Dei*: Adam and God are very similar in their physical appearance and there is an almost exact correspondence between them: eyes, shoulders, arms, waist, legs, feet and toes. Adam's concave body shape is an echo of God's convex body shape. This all points to the idea that we are made *imago Dei*, in the image of God, creatures who reflect God in the world.

- Yet God is ineffable: Michelangelo was not daft and knew that God's true nature lies beyond the descriptions of any artist, writer or speaker. However, the artist can try to capture ways in which we 'image God', and if we look carefully, we will see that Michelangelo has placed God inside a brain-shaped cloud. Perhaps Michelangelo is saying that God is the source of all intelligence, knowledge and wisdom, and that he shares this with us and makes us in the image of the divine life.

- The Feminine: people have speculated who is in the brain-shaped cloud with God.

  Is the nervous-looking person under God's left arm Eve, not yet created, but already present in the Mind of God the Creator, already part of his eternal plan, because human beings are not made for loneliness, but for relationship and love, mirroring God?

  Is it Mary, the 'New Eve' in her special place next to God, with Christ her child on the left? If this is correct, we are being reminded by Michelangelo that Jesus will in due time come like a new Adam to restore human beings in God's image (Romans 5:12–18).

- Beauty and goodness: this beautiful painting on the ceiling of a beautiful chapel contains well-defined, handsome figures. Adam has youthful good looks, while God has more of a grizzled ruggedness about him! Remember that Genesis 1 says, over and over and over again, that Creation is good and beauty is one of the ways in which the eternal touches the temporary and in wonder we are given a glimpse of God.

Discussion

Take a visual tour of the Sistine Chapel: **http://www.vatican.va/various/cappelle/index_sistina_en.htm**. What features of it strike you? Is art a better way of expressing faith and religious feelings than using words?

In this unit we explore the idea of the Tree of Life, once withered through the sin of Adam, but flourishing again as the New Tree of Life, the Cross of Christ, who is the Last Adam (1 Corinthians 15:45; see also Romans 5:12–18).

Human Communication: the spiritual through the physical

As we have seen, Catholics believe that human beings are both body and soul, material and spiritual, earth-bound (made of the soil) and divine (with the breath of life). This has consequences for the way we communicate:

'In human life signs and symbols occupy an important place. As a being at once body and spirit, man expresses and perceives spiritual realities through physical signs and symbols. As a social being, man needs signs and symbols to communicate with others, through language, gestures, and actions. The same holds true for his relationship with God.'

CCC 1146

Spiritual (and therefore invisible) realities – thoughts, emotions, feelings, love – have to be expressed externally not just in words but in gestures and actions. That is why love gives rise to so many artistic expressions in paintings, songs, plays, films, books and poems! It is also why people often express love by exchanging gifts or sharing a meal. Hence the Church hands on its testimony, its witness to Jesus, by using many signs, symbols and images.

Symbols

- What is a symbol? , Cardinal Avery Dulles says that a symbol is "an externally perceived sign that suggests more than it can clearly describe or define." (The Symbolic Structure of Revelation, p. 55)

- What does he mean by this? Well at one level signs are all round us helping us find directions when we travel and they are very necessary. Some may point to something such the MacDonalds 'M' arches which suggest: 'Yum Yum: Food is here!'

- However, when we come to the flags of different countries - we are dealing with more than mere colours and cloth. These are symbols which mean a great deal to people and denote identity, history, culture and belonging.

- Taking this a step further into the religious realm, symbols are often used to express mysteries because they can take us beyond words into our heart and imagination. They are more than signs because they have an abundance of meaning for us.

Sign = something that points to something else.

Symbol = a non-verbal sign of something.

Pantokrator = Greek for 'Almighty'.

Evangelists = authors of the four Gospels of Matthew, Mark, Luke and John.

◦ Think of a friend or a relative that we call to mind through a memento, a gift or a ring –the symbol may be small but it can represent the whole mystery of a person we love. No wonder then that in religious art, symbols are often used to express the infinite mystery of God?

The 'Tree of Life' Mosaic

For the GCSE, the challenge is to study a classic example of Christian symbolism, so we have chosen the 'Tree of Life' mosaic from the Church of San Clemente in Rome. As the old saying goes, a picture paints a thousand words – but, taking the four key themes in turn, we'll keep it down to about 800, with a 200-word summary!

The Cross

◦ Cross as Life. In the centre, Christ appears on a black cross. But, as G. K. Chesterton explains, his face is 'radiant and like the sun at noon' because this mosaic is an image of life, not death. The hand of God, above the cross, takes the cross and 'thrust[s] it into the earth below … but its touch is not death but life'. The cross is the tree of life. This idea is emphasised because at the base of the cross stands a tree, a symbol of the tree of life in Genesis 2:9 (also known as the tree of the knowledge of good and evil).

◦ Cross as Forgiveness. It is a mystery in itself that an instrument of execution has become for Christians a sign of hope, yet this is what a symbol can do. Sin associated with Adam and Eve who disobeyed God and ate from the forbidden tree is forgiven because Jesus gave his life for humanity on the tree of the cross.

◦ Cross and the Apostles: The twelve doves (a symbol of the Spirit of God) perched on the Cross are symbols of the twelve apostles who were filled with the Holy Spirit (Acts 2). The apostles are also portrayed as twelve sheep around the bottom of the mosaic, facing Jesus who, as the Lamb of God, hangs at the centre of the Cross (Revelation 21:14).

The Vine

The Vine as Christ: there is a lush, green vine that winds all around the mosaic which is a symbol of Jesus, who said, 'I am the Vine' (John 15:5).

The Vine as Church: the inscription on the mosaic says: 'We will compare the Church of Christ to this vine'. The Church only has life through Christ and is a sacrament for the world. Mary and John (either side of the Cross), as well as the nobles, peasants about their daily work, Fathers of the Church, saints and prophets, are symbolic of the fact that the Church is meant to include everyone.

Paradise and Redemption

- ° Heaven on Earth: the abundant green life is meant to remind us of the Garden of Eden, the origins of the human race and our relationship with God, who walks with Adam and Eve in the garden (Genesis 3:8). Ancient Romans connected trees, green plants and palm branches with the gods. This link between gardens, trees, plants, vines, palms and Heaven continued in early Christian art.

- ° Eden/Paradise: these themes are also represented beneath Christ's Cross, from which a river flows (see Genesis 2:10–14). Where the river divides, we see deer quenching their thirst, like the soul thirsting for God in Psalm 42:1. There is also the scary presence of a serpent – a symbol of the temptation which led to Adam's original sin (Genesis 3:1–8) – which wraps itself around a fawn that is drinking from the rivers of life. This is symbol of how sin tries to ruin our life with God and can spoil our life in this world.

- ° Overcoming Evil: for some reason, Ancient Romans used to hang rags on trees to 'keep in' with the gods and win good fortune and to keep the forces of evil at bay. In this mosaic, Christ is hung out by the human race like a scruffy rag on the tree of the Cross, overcoming all evil and achieving an everlasting good.

- ° A World Redeemed: Christ's blood was poured out on the Cross to redeem human beings from original sin, and we see a symbol of this spilling of blood in the Church, especially in the Eucharist. The Lamb's blood in the vine reaches even Jupiter and Neptune, ancient gods of Rome – suggesting, controversially perhaps, that Christ's sacrifice redeems all, including pagans and those who lived before him in history.

- ° Bethlehem and Jerusalem: as the places associated with the beginning and end of Jesus' life, these are both represented. Bethlehem is on the left, with Jesus as a boy running with another boy, and, above the town, the Old Testament prophet Isaiah, together with St Lawrence and St Paul; and Jerusalem is on the right, symbolised by the cock that crew as Peter denied Jesus.

The Almighty

Transcendence: the hand of God the Father surrounded by clouds and stars, symbolic of the *transcendent God* reaching down to earth from beyond the cosmos, from heaven. He becomes the *immanent God* in Jesus, handing a crown to Christ and giving him the power to redeem us through the Cross.

Pantokrator: at the very top of the mosaic we see Christ *Pantokrator* (= omnipotent/all-powerful), a symbol that the Jesus of the Cross is also the risen Son of God and Supreme Judge of the universe, with the words: 'Glory to God in heaven seated on his throne and on earth peace to people of good will'.

Gospels: here also the four evangelists are symbolised by the winged man (Matthew), the lion (Mark), the ox (Luke) and the eagle (John).

Jesus

In the Apse mosaic there are also other more abstract symbols which are representations of Jesus. These are the *Chi-Rho* and the *Alpha* and *Omega*. These two symbols are combined in one monogram at the top of the mosaic. Monograms are symbols made up of letters or initials. And when these monograms are used to refer to Christ, they are called Christograms. All of the early Christian symbols used letters from the Greek alphabet because this was the language shared by most of the different cultures and language groups in the many different parts of the Roman Empire at the time of the early Christians.

At the top of the mosaic you will see the first two letters of the word Christ in Greek (ΧΡΙΣΤΟΣ) and these are combined into a Christogram called the *Chi-Rho* (the name of the two letters in Greek). This symbol is still a common symbol in Catholic churches today and is often featured on baptismal candles, priestly vestments and sacred vessels. The letter which looks like an X, is actually the first letter of the word Christ in Greek (equivalent to English "Ch" as it is pronounced in "loch"). And the letter which looks like a P, is actually the second letter of the word Christ in Greek (equivalent to the English "R").

On either side of the *Chi-Rho* is another set of letters used as a symbol of Christ which comes from the scriptures. The book of Revelation uses the symbolism of the Greek letters alpha and omega several times. Alpha and Omega (A and Ω) are the first and last letters of the Greek alphabet and the phrase was common at the time of Jesus to express the sense of something being complete (we still use this in English when we talk of knowing things A to Z). In the book of Revelation God speaks of himself as the "Alpha and Omega," and from the very earliest times Christians understood the title to refer to Jesus also. It is another way of speaking about Jesus as sharing the eternity of God.

Summary of the Symbolism

- The whole cosmos was created by God the Father through the Word of God.
- In time that Word became flesh in Jesus of Nazareth. He died to redeem sinful human beings on the wood of the Cross, which is therefore the tree of life.
- Jesus is also the Risen Lord, the all-powerful Judge of the universe that was created through him (Colossians 1:16).
- He is how humans find their meaning. The loving God who created us and who is the Father of us all seeks to unite us in Christ through the community of the Church as one family. Although sin divides us and turns us against one another, humanity must not forget its common origin in God and its destiny in God (Colossians 1:17).
- The victory of Christ has to be accepted in the life of each of us. The mosaic invites those who look at it to ponder its rich symbols and enter into the mystery of God, creation, and the battle between good and evil. It boldly asks which side we are on: are we for Life or for Death?

Discussion

Jesus as Lived Symbol

Although God is a spiritual, invisible reality, communication with us involves using physical realities: words which we can hear, read and understand; gestures which we can see; or actions which we can see and understand. Of course, the supreme way in which God does this is in Jesus, his Word of love made flesh, who spoke, performed deeds and was God's love in action:

'Something which has existed since the beginning, that we have heard, and we have seen with our own eyes; that we have watched and touched with our hands: the Word, who is life – this is our subject. That life was made visible: we saw it and are giving our testimony, telling you of the eternal life which was with the Father and has been made visible to us'.

1 John 1:1–2

Would you agree that ultimately deeds are more important than words? Whose life do you find inspiring and 'symbolic' of what you would like to do or be?

Unit 1.15a: *Imago Dei* and Catholic Social Teaching

CORE IDEA

In this unit we look at how the notion of God as Creator and the concept of humanity as *imago Dei* in turn influence Catholic Social Teaching about justice, peace and reconciliation.

Creation belongs to Everyone!

Understood in the religious sense, for Catholics (as well as other Christians, together with Muslims and Jews), Genesis tells the truth that God is Creator of everything, that creation is 'good' (Genesis 1:31) and that human beings were made in the image and likeness of God and given the task of caring for creation. Catholics call this task 'stewardship of Creation'.

'Yahweh God took the man and settled him in the garden of Eden to cultivate and take care of it.'

Genesis 2:15

KEY TERMS

Catholic Social Teaching = Church guidelines on how society should foster human dignity. Laudato Si' – the 2015 letter by Pope Francis on care of the environment.

TASK

Watch and discuss the universe creation story as told in the 2014 film Noah. What truths can you find in it?

BAKOUNINE / Shutterstock.com

Increasingly we realise that, like the man helped by the Good Samaritan, creation is wounded and needs our care.

To care for creation means to protect and conserve it using the earth's resources in a sustainable way. This benefits both the earth itself and human beings, especially the poorest people in less economically developed countries, who are the most affected by climate change even though they have done the least to cause it. Acting sustainably also means that the earth's resources will still be there to benefit future generations.

For Catholics, considering those who are poorest and most vulnerable first – known as the Option for the Poor – is always part of protecting the environment. Pope Francis says that peace, justice and preservation of creation cannot be separated; every attempt to preserve ecology must also take account of the rights of the poorest and most vulnerable people (*Laudato Si'* 92–93).

Imago Dei and Catholic Social Teaching

We have seen how the Bible and great Christian thinkers like St Catherine of Siena have emphasised the importance of the *imago Dei*. This has led to the Church developing guidelines for putting it into practice, that are generally referred to as Catholic Social Teaching.

In practice, down through the centuries, members of the Catholic Church have given some selfless examples of respecting the dignity of each person through their service of others. Since the earliest days of the Church, when poorer members of the community were given special consideration (Acts 2:45), justice and charity have been integral to how committed Catholics have lived their faith, and many saints and Church leaders have left inspired writings about this.

But in 1891, when Pope Leo XIII wrote his encyclical, On Capital and Labour (Rerum Novarum), Catholic teaching on social issues began to be recorded more systematically. Since then, many popes have reflected on the social issues of their day, in the light of Scripture and the lived experience of God's people. Along with other documents written by bishops, saints and leaders of the early Church, these writings have become known as 'Catholic Social Teaching'.

From 1962 to 1965, the world's bishops gathered in Rome for the Second Vatican Council to discuss and make decisions on Church teachings. One Council document, *Gaudium et Spes*, which looked at the Church in the modern world, made it clear that the concept of the image of God (*imago Dei*) has greatly influenced Church teaching on human dignity, equality, justice and peace:

'Since all men possess a rational soul and **are created in God's likeness**, since they have the same nature and origin, have been redeemed by Christ and enjoy the same divine calling and destiny, **the basic equality of all** must receive increasingly greater recognition…

…**excessive economic and social differences** between the members of the one human family or population groups cause scandal, and **militate against social justice, equity, the dignity of the human person**, as well as social and international **peace**.'

Gaudium et Spes 29

To ponder

If I fully believed that the person next to me is an image of God, how would I treat him or her?

This last teaching from *Gaudium et Spes* makes the link between justice and international peace very clear. Catholic teaching says that peace between peoples and nations is not possible unless justice exists first. In fact, it goes so far as to say that the absence of war is not the same as true peace:

'Peace is not merely the absence of war; ... Instead, it is ... an enterprise of justice... This peace on earth cannot be obtained unless personal well-being is safeguarded and people freely and trustingly share with one another the riches of their inner spirits and their talents ... Hence peace is likewise the fruit of love, which goes beyond what justice can provide'

Gaudium et Spes 78

Case study: Father Pacho

During Colombia's fifty years of armed conflict, thousands have died and more than six million people have been forced from their homes.

Father Francisco de Roux SJ / www.indcatholicnews.com

When he was the director of CAFOD partner CINEP, Father Francisco de Roux SJ (known as 'Pacho') brokered a peace agreement between the Colombian government and the M-19 guerrilla movement. He is never afraid to uncover the truth and speaks out for human rights even if this puts him at great personal danger. At one point he was captured and sentenced to execution.

At the heart of Father Pacho's message is the need for dialogue and a peaceful solution to the armed conflict. Yet Father Pacho considers the root of Colombia's crisis to be a spiritual problem:

'Our problem wasn't economic or political. It was ... the destruction of our dignity; the absence of the recognition of who we are ... [and of] the dignity we have just because we are human beings.'

In 2012, Colombian peace negotiations began in Havana, Cuba. Father Pacho went to Havana with 60 survivors of the conflict who had been kidnapped or raped or who had survived massacres, to tell their stories to the negotiators. He described it as a moment of profound transformation in the dialogue.

It was hoped that by late 2016 a peace agreement could be signed – a first step towards reconciliation and lasting peace.

Discussion

- Why might hearing from survivors face to face have profoundly transformed the Colombian negotiations?
- How is *imago Dei* linked to justice, peace and reconciliation?
- *Gaudium et Spes* 78 says: 'A firm determination to respect other men and peoples and their dignity, as well as the studied practice of brotherhood, are absolutely necessary for the establishment of peace.' Explain why this might be so.

Unit 1.15b: The Work of CAFOD and the SVP

CORE IDEA

The extent to which the work of one Catholic charity, such as CAFOD and one local charity, such as SVP, reflect Catholic beliefs about the dignity of human beings, the importance of loving one's neighbour, and respecting creation.

CAFOD The Catholic Fund for Overseas Development (CAFOD) is the official aid agency of the Catholic Church in England and Wales. It works through the local Catholic Church and other partners in Africa, Asia, Latin America and the Middle East to fight poverty and injustice, wherever the need is greatest.

Although it is a mega-organisation nowadays, it started in ordinary homes when volunteer members of the National Board of Catholic Women organised the first Family Fast Day in 1960. Two years later, CAFOD was born.

CAFOD and Dignity

Dignity is a key principle of Catholic Social Teaching; it is also one of CAFOD's key values: 'We believe in the intrinsic dignity of every person. We work with all people regardless of race, gender, religion or politics.'

CAFOD says that part of its vision is a world where 'the rights and dignity of every person are respected'.

For example, CAFOD's Dennis Momoh organised teams of brave volunteers in Sierra Leone, giving safe, dignified burials to people who had died of Ebola during the outbreak in 2014–15.

Dennis Momoh/ CAFOD

'Dignity is at the heart of the burial team… family members are concerned about the way their loved ones are being buried,' Dennis said.

'We ensure that before somebody is buried, prayers are said. We also ensure that family members can follow from a distance, so that they have the opportunity to bid farewell to their loved ones.'

CAFOD and Neighbours

When a lawyer asked, 'And who is my neighbour?', Jesus told him the story of the Good Samaritan showing neighbourly love to a wounded man from another culture who had nothing with which to repay the favour (Luke 10:25–37). At the end of the parable, Jesus said, 'Go, and do the same yourself.'

'Neighbour' need not be restricted to local people. Pope Benedict XVI wrote the following:

KEY TERMS

CAFOD = Catholic Fund for Overseas Development.

SVP = St Vincent de Paul Society.

Preferential Option for the Poor = a guiding principle of Catholic Social Teaching.

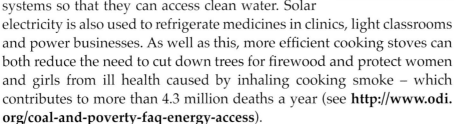

'Anyone who needs me, and whom I can help, is my neighbour. The concept of "neighbour" is now universalised, yet it remains concrete. Despite being extended to all mankind, it is not reduced to a generic, abstract and undemanding expression of love, but calls for my own practical commitment here and now.'

Deus Caritas Est 15

CAFOD gives Catholics in England and Wales opportunities to reach out to their neighbours in other countries – by making lifestyle choices that respect the planet and its poorest people, by praying, by campaigning for justice and by fundraising.

CAFOD and Creation

The Catholic Social Teaching principle 'stewardship of creation' is integral to CAFOD's work. CAFOD aims to promote human development while also protecting and sustaining the environment.

Solar power enables irrigation of a greenhouse in Isiolo, Kenya/ CAFOD

For example, CAFOD's work in Kenya shows how solar electricity can help people lift themselves out of poverty – for instance, by helping people to pump water to grow more food, both to feed their families and to sell, and powering water-filtering systems so that they can access clean water. Solar electricity is also used to refrigerate medicines in clinics, light classrooms and power businesses. As well as this, more efficient cooking stoves can both reduce the need to cut down trees for firewood and protect women and girls from ill health caused by inhaling cooking smoke – which contributes to more than 4.3 million deaths a year (see **http://www.odi.org/coal-and-poverty-faq-energy-access**).

The St Vincent de Paul Society

The St Vincent de Paul Society (SVP) is an international voluntary Christian organisation started in Paris in 1833 by Blessed Frédéric Ozanam and his companions. Inspired by St Vincent de Paul, in the spirit of justice and charity it seeks to help those who are suffering from poverty of any sort.

Most SVP groups, called 'conferences', are based in parishes, but there are also groups in primary and secondary schools and in universities.

The SVP and Dignity

The Fundamental Principles of the Society of Saint Vincent de Paul say that the Society's work 'involves all forms of aid by individual contact in order to promote the dignity and integrity of man'.

Individual visits to people who are sick, lonely, addicted, imprisoned or coping with disability form a large proportion of the Society's work. SVP members aim to ensure that every person visited knows that he or she is valued and respected as an individual, and that there is someone they can turn to for a helping hand or a sympathetic ear.

An essential mandate of the Society's work is to provide help while taking care to maintain the confidentiality and dignity of those who are served.

The SVP and Neighbours

Vincent de Paul said: 'God does not consider the outcome of the good work undertaken but the charity that accompanied it'.

The SVP says that its vision is inspired by Christ's message to love our neighbour as ourselves. The Society is non-judgemental about those asking for assistance – it will help anyone in need, as long as the local membership is able to do so.

St Vincent/ svp.org.uk

In some areas, an SVP support centre, community shop or furniture store serves the most disadvantaged people in the neighbourhood.

The SVP and Creation

One way of protecting creation is to choose to recycle rather than waste resources.

SVP furniture centres repair donated pieces of furniture that are damaged and redistribute the repaired items to people who have need of them. This practical action combines stewardship of creation with neighbourly love. (See **http://svp.org.uk/Projects**)

Discussion

'In the end, only kindness matters'

Jewel Kilcher

Read Matthew 25:31–46. How does this fit with either (a) Catholic Social Teaching, (b) the work of CAFOD, or (c) the work of SVP? Do you think your parish, your school or you could be more involved in such initiatives? How?

TASK

Locate your nearest SVP Conference and invite one of its members to tell your class about its work.